More Letters from the Country

More Letters from the Country

by
Marsha Boulton

Little, Brown and Company (Canada) Limited
Boston • New York • Toronto • London

FIRST PRINTING

Canadian Cataloguing in Publication Data

Boulton, Marsha
More letters from the country

1st Canadian ed.
ISBN 0–316–10238–5

1. Farm life – Ontario – Anecdotes. I. Title.

S522.C3B68 1997   630'.9713   C97–930375–3

Jacket Design by TANIA CRAAN

Cover Photograph by JOHN REEVES

Interior Design and Page Composition by JOSEPH GISINI
OF ANDREW SMITH GRAPHICS, INC.

Printed and bound in Canada by BEST BOOK MANUFACTURERS

LITTLE, BROWN AND COMPANY (CANADA) LIMITED
148 YORKVILLE AVENUE,
TORONTO, ON, CANADA, M5R 1C2

10 9 8 7 6 5 4 3 2 1

Table of Contents

Spring

Summer

Fall

Winter

Foreword

WHEN *LETTERS FROM THE COUNTRY* WAS AWARDED the Stephen Leacock Medal for Humour one of my neighbours told me not to let it go to my head.

"After all," she said, "didn't they give a pig named Babe an Academy Award?"

Living in the country helps you keep your sense of things straight. Later, when I was signing books at my local Stedmans store during the height of the 1996 Summer Olympics I let a boy of about eleven years hold the solid-silver Leacock Medal. He began tossing it casually in the air to feel its weight. When he palmed it back to me, he said, "Gee, just think, if you'd swum faster, you would have beat that Irish girl and got the gold."

Humour is the observation of an unprejudiced heart. It does not hit you in the face like a cream pie. It reveals itself in tickles of irony stroked by insight. Stephen Leacock himself suggested that it might be "the mingled heritage of tears and laughter that is our common lot on earth." I could not agree more. Mr. Leacock also fancied himself a farmer.

He once tried raising turkeys on linoleum to solve the problem of cleaning mucky pens. Say no more.

More Letters from the Country is not what you would call an original title, but that is exactly what this collection represents. I hope it gives reviewers something to comment upon without confusing readers with something that it is not. When nature and human nature synthesize, there are bound to be stories. The farm and its community are constant sources of inspiration and pathos.

Since the publication of *Letters from the Country*, I have met many urbanites who are considering a rural transition. Some are serious about farming; others just want to enjoy the crunch of their own organic carrots and the crow of a rooster in the morning. I see myself in their enthusiasm, and I know that their dreams are not for tempering. They tell me that they understand it will not be easy and they are ready for hard work.

Inevitably, I discover that they all have some ambitious self-portrait that forms a back-of-the-eyeball sentimental painting of what country life will be like for them. It could be a family scene straight out of *The Waltons*. It could be a James Herriot-type Hallmark greeting card. It could even be a virtual reality hologram of standing at the manger on Christmas Eve in a moment of pure contentment. I know where they are coming from, having conjured such images myself and discovered that they can, sometimes, find form.

No doubt, novitiates will encounter the inevitable tragedy that accompanies animal husbandry, and the vexing variables of weather and other weevils, but I admire their collective spirit of adventure. Their neighbours will be watching, as country neighbours do. Hopefully, they will find in their community as generous a spirit as I have found in my mine. Hopefully, they will learn from their mistakes and hold steady to the positive.

Country life is not for everyone. For that matter, most of us will never spend a summer in the south of France, but we enjoy reading about what it might be like. I have met many people who are perfectly content to maintain an armchair-reader's distance from stupid sheep tricks and the travails of haying or the physicality of barnyard midwifery. There are times when I wish I could join them.

Farmers — real farmers, present and past — have a natural suspicion of any outsider who attempts to translate their world. Too often, they are portrayed as "complainers." On April 3, 1979, Prime Minister Pierre Trudeau said of farmers: "When there is too much sun, they complain. When there is too much rain, they complain. A farmer is a complainer." Well, Mr. Trudeau lost that election but he remained well fed by the complainers, as did the nation.

Today's farmers — male and female — must contend with environmental issues and global marketplaces, along with local politics and straightening the blade on the plough. One hundred fertile acres cannot be guaranteed to provide for a family as they once did. Even with specialization and genetic manipulation and irradiation, there are no guarantees. Panaceas and technology cannot replace the instinct of farmers.

Instead of a mixture of livestock and crops, all of the eggs tend to be placed in one basket and scrambled into something that barely resembles real food. Instead of being a place of purity, chemical residue and pollution put farmers in a battle against the very land they live on. Instead of passing from one generation to another, the farm is often passed to the bank.

So, I have been pleased when farmers tell me that my stories put them to sleep at night. This might not seem like the accolade most writers would treasure. However, when you know how hard farmers work in a day and the stresses they are under, it is a great compliment to be granted any moment of their time.

I was speaking to a businesswomen's gathering and I met a spunky senior entrepreneur.

"I was you forty years ago," she said. "A city girl all my life until I married a farmer. I did all the dumb things you did and I'm glad I did them, too."

She went on to tell me about her first farm garden. Like me, she planted every seed she could lay her hands on and waited to see what would happen. But when it came time to harvest her turnips, she hid them from her new mate.

"I thought I'd done something terribly wrong," she confided. "My turnips were nice and round, but they didn't have a lick of wax on them."

I have heard many such stories since then. They include the one about the fat lady who got stuck in the outhouse with the beehive. Sometimes there really is nothing more to say.

— MARSHA BOULTON

Acknowledgements

OCCASIONALLY PEOPLE ASK ME IF MY STORIES ARE TRUE. Television crews have gone so far as to interview my neighbours to find out. Even my publisher, Kim McArthur, checked up on me by bringing her children to watch The World's Largest All-Female Marching Kazoo Band in action. I must, therefore, thank my neighbours and my community for being exactly as they are, because creating them would be impossible. The motto painted on the water tower of the Town of Mount Forest pretty much says it all: "High, Healthy and Happy." Maybe it is something in the southwestern Ontario water supply, but I suspect it is universal.

Following the publication of *Letters from the Country* I heard from many people who had known me in previous high-heeled incarnations and marvelled at my transition to Wellington boots. I also heard from my Grade Three teacher. Mrs. Briggs wrote a touching letter in which she recalled remarkable details of my suburban learning experience, including the position of my school desk, "on the blackboard side of Room Thirteen."

Thus prompted, I checked my Grade Three report card and discovered this cryptic comment from Mrs. Briggs on my first-semester progress: "Marsha is an energetic and willing worker, but must learn to work by herself." The fact is, I recall spending most of that semester working at my desk in the school corridor because of a propensity for telling stories out of turn.

I must thank Mrs. Briggs and all of the other educators who channelled my energy. Their lessons were well taught and well learned, since writing is work that one does in a resounding solitude.

I also thank my father, Geoff, whose note back to Mrs. Briggs read: "Please define 'work by herself.'" He and my mother, Marg, taught me to understand a phrase before turning it lightly.

For the benefit of CBC Radio's *Fresh Air* listeners, who follow my rural antics through "farm letter" readings by host Tom Allen, I will answer the question that I am most often asked when I make personal contact with a program fan. Please be advised that Tom looks like a cross between Robert Redford in *Butch Cassidy and the Sundance Kid* and Tom Hanks in *Big*. And, yes, he is as charming as he sounds.

To acknowledge the goodwill of my literary agent Bruce Westwood and his colleagues at Westwood Creative Artists, I have chosen *not* to tell the story of Mr. Westwood's wild-flower-pasture-planting fiasco.

Likewise, I am beholden to all of the faithful at Little, Brown who serve the demands of many authors — not to mention myself and Marianne Faithful. Under the guiding baton of General McArthur, I am certain all of you soldiers of the book would make a mindboggling marching kazoo band. I salute you troops, particularly for the wise counsel you kept with regard to the virtually unthawable legs of lamb I delivered last year three hours before the Little, Brown–*Morningside* barbecue. Do not think for a minute that your discretion has gone unnoticed.

Finally, my heartfelt thanks to Stephen Williams for granting me a special dispensation to tell Moose-tales that would make a lesser man blush.

Spring

Sold on Nirvana

*W*HEN PEOPLE ASK ME WHY I TRADED CITY LIFE FOR life in the country, I always feel that I should have some reasoned and well-thought-out explanation. Instead, I blame it all on a real estate agent who caught me in a romantic moment and played on that vision until I signed on the dotted line.

In years of talking to urban transplants much like myself, I find that I am not alone. The real estate agent I am referring to has become something of a legend.

We call him "The Boss Hog," because in some ways he resembles the portly character who once appeared on a really bad, Cracker-Jack-box of a television series called *The Dukes of Hazzard*. Our Boss Hog also has that streak of unctuousness that seems to flow naturally from the personality of all really good sales people.

Just like the funeral director who can fit you to a casket while you are still standing, the Boss Hog can figure out what sort of gem of a property you really need in that instant when you pause before the pictures displayed in his

Main Street office window. Somehow he manages to cajole shy people — street-proofed people and people who check their children's Halloween apples for razor-blades — to jump into his big shiny Buick and go for a ride. Something about him makes strangers believe that he can lead them to nirvana, and it is just around the corner.

There are, of course, tricks to the trade. Some back roads look better than others. If the Boss Hog is trying to sell a country lot to someone who wants to build their dream log cabin in a sylvan glade, he won't take them along the route past the gravel pit down the road. No, he will drive along a winding wooded concession, where other log cabins are barely visible through the cedar trees and the silence is only broken by the chatter of pheasants in the bush.

If you are looking for a property that has a stream running through it, he will drive you along a route that has a seemingly endless number of bridges that all pass over a babbling brook.

Perhaps, he will stop to point out a secret trout hole where the river curls around the roots of willow trees. This works best in the early spring when the banks are gushing with clear cold water, or in the fall after the mosquitos and black flies have gone to rest.

It seems water has a great appeal to most people who are thinking of country life, but not every property actually has a river running through it.

That is no problem for the Boss Hog.

"You're better off starting from scratch," he will say. And from then on the words to watch for are: "This one has an ideal pond site."

Virtually everyone he sells a property to believes that an underground Amazon of water is flowing just beneath the surface of their land, waiting to be tapped and transformed into a picture-perfect, spring-fed pond.

The Boss Hog never takes you past the places where muddy holes in the ground have been waiting for years for water to fill them. But he can recommend a douser who is so proficient at finding water with a witching rod that he can locate the indoor plumbing in any house without even asking for directions.

There are always lots of properties on the market in the country. But if the Boss Hog has his way, you might be led to think that Eden is almost all sold-out.

I have friends who bought a glorious old stone farmhouse several years ago with every intention of making it a permanent residence. They poured a ton of money into reconstructing the gingerbread trim, creating the perfect wrap-around porch and landscaping with a riot of wild flowers to complement the whole she-bang. Things change, and their jobs have overtaken the dream. They make it out to the country for a few weeks each summer, and at Christmastime the whole family comes up to do the Currier and Ives stuff, but otherwise the place is vacant.

It came as quite a surprise when the urban owners showed up one weekend unexpectedly to enjoy the autumn leaves. There, on the front lawn, was a large real estate sign from the Boss Hog's emporium and across it was a big red "SOLD" sticker. Naturally, the Boss Hog had a simple explanation — just a mistake someone in the office made. The sign disappeared into his trunk, along with a bunch of others.

That is another trick of the trade.

Once you are trapped in that Buick, the "SOLD" signs seem to be everywhere, all of them the product of the Boss Hog. By the time you get to the dilapidated old place that needs a new roof and some severe work done on the septic system, the Boss Hog has you in his cross-hairs believing that it may just be the last place on earth that is ever going to come up for grabs.

"There aren't many of these beauties left," he will say, pointing out the hardwood floor underneath the linoleum and scraping the painted banister to show you the cherry wood underneath layers of aged paint.

Anyone will tell you that if you buy an older home there is bound to be some renovation, restoration and redecorating involved. The Boss Hog can make it sound like an adventure. All of a sudden you feel like Martha Stewart. Visions of frilly country curtains and flower-box herb gardens dance in your head. The bleak, fly-specked wallpaper in every room becomes a blank canvas upon which you will sponge paint and appliqué yourself into heaven on earth. Every dark space with a roof over its head seems to be a perfect candidate for a skylight. There is no end to the possibilities.

Next thing you know, you are signing on the dotted line and the "SOLD" sign becomes a reality.

Buying the rural dream and living it turn out to be two separate realities, but true to the Boss Hog's word, it is an adventure.

I am actually glad I took the drive in the big old Buick all those years ago. One of these days, I expect I will get around to finding the underground river beneath my perfect pond site. Every few years, I pull up some ancient linoleum and finish a few more feet of hardwood floor to a gleaming polish. There is plenty of time to shape nirvana to my liking. Who needs another leaky skylight?

At least with the Boss Hog watching, I will know when I have achieved perfection.

One day, I will come home unexpectedly and find a "SOLD" sign at the end of the lane. The Boss Hog will tell me it was planted in error, but I will know that all of my effort has finally elevated me to "country gem" status.

In the meantime, I think I'll just enjoy the endless possibilities that have no explanation.

Just the Facts

I MIGHT HAVE BEEN AS GREEN AS A CORN SPROUT WHEN I came to the farm, but I had a lot of ideas. After all, I had managed to purchase a one-hundred-acre farm without any fencing. There was no barn, just one little shed built near a swamp and a rickety old chicken coop close to the house. As a farm, the whole thing was not much more than an idea.

While disentangling myself from urban life, I spent weekends in the country studying books and creating game plans. I asked the government for information, and huge envelopes started arriving. Each one contained some sort of single-page, agricultural fact sheet. Page by page, the mystery of farming was revealed.

When I was ready to get down to it, I called in a government specialist to review my plan. This procedure was pro forma according to fact sheet 96.

A nice man came to the door and shuffled his feet when I asked him to come in. On the kitchen table I had a pile of books about sheep and a rough map of the farm and where I thought things should go. A look of panic crossed his face, but it eased when my companion, the Moose, came through the door. Moose is a large, genial fellow. They shook hands and nodded in a manly way. Then Moose left the room.

Panic reconfigured on the specialist's face when I explained that the farm was *my* operation. The Moose would continue working in the city until such time as the bounty of the farm provided a living. According to fact sheet 33, this might take five years, unless I fast-tracked the sheep according to Accelerated Breeding Plan B in fact sheet 56, which was my Plan A.

We started out by examining land-base strategies. The specialist suggested share cropping the hay and grain fields. Details of this procedure were spelled out in fact sheet 16. Since I had no machinery for planting or harvesting or much of anything really, it made sense. Besides, fact sheet 82 indicated that I would need to have a storage area for machinery and a well-lit area for making repairs, but that would have to wait until I had a barn.

I was not surprised when my barn plan passed muster with the specialist. It was taken directly from fact sheet 65 — "Loose Housing For Sheep." My only modification was an annotation along the front wall for a gallery that would contain various posters, needlepoints and other forms of art depicting sheep. Fact sheet 21 said that a barn should be designed to make the farmer comfortable, as well as the livestock. A variety of visual images in the barn would brighten my day. I was halfway through a needlepoint of grazing sheep.

When it came to fencing, the specialist seemed quite

impressed by my combination of materials. Fact sheet 43 said flexibility was key to farming. The hard lines on my map indicated page-wire fence, the dotted lines were for electric fencing to divide pastures, and the ziggy lines were for picturesque cedar rail fencing near the house.

Fence posts could be cut from the forest, which counted as Woodlot Management according to fact sheet 79. The short-stop on Moose's baseball team would do the job. He was also an experienced tree-cutter. After reading fact sheet 80 about safety in the bush, bringing in an expert seemed prudent.

Fact sheet 52 talked about admitting your limitations, so I admitted that I would also be hiring someone to install the fences. I had not known who to hire until Irving, the handyman who washed the second-storey windows on the house, told me that he knew a guy who had a tractor and a fence puller. His name was Bo and he was a retired circus clown, but Irving said he was good at straight lines. I also had a backhoe operator lined up to dig the post holes because the ground was Class 6 soil — in other words, solid rock.

By this time we had downed two pots of tea and barely a word had been spoken about sheep. In accordance with the general instruction on "Planning Your Sheep Operation," I presented my flow chart. Based on a fifty-fifty ratio of female to male lambs at one and a half lambs per ewe on a breeding cycle of three lambings over thirty-two months I estimated that my core group of twenty ewes would multiply to a flock of 175 within five years. I knew that was optimistic, but fact sheet 104 said a positive attitude was a prerequisite to farming.

Then I waited for advice.

"Do you have a wheelbarrow?" the specialist asked.

I told him I did — a fine, big, blue one.

"Good," he said. "Fill it up with money and you can start farming."

Almost twenty years later, the clown-built fence is still standing and the needlepoint on the barn wall always gives me great pleasure. There are fewer sheep to feed now than there were after the first five years, but there is also less land to share crop since the stony ground became a gravel pit. Although it is not a full-time job, the woodlot is now managed by Moose. He says it will be ready to harvest when we are ready to retire. We call it the RRSP forest.

Oh yes, I still have the blue wheelbarrow. I could not have farmed without it. Every time I have a new idea, I ask myself, "Will that be one wheelbarrow full or two?"

There really should be a fact sheet about that.

The Kindergarten Ducks

PEOPLE ARE ALWAYS TRYING TO GIVE YOU STUFF WHEN you live in the country. When you first move, country people try to fob off their old junk on you. I had one neighbour who had been collecting old wooden doors for no apparent reason. When he found out I had sheep, he brought over a wagon load for me to use as pen dividers. He just dumped them off and left, as though (1) I needed the doors and (2) I knew what to do with them.

My city friends seem to think that my farm is a retirement home for any pets they do not want, or cannot take care of anymore. I have had everything from a Siamese cat that ate its owner's tropical fish to a hundred-pound Japanese huskie that grew up in a beauty salon. Both animals were terrified of sheep. They got used to it. I like to think that their twilight years were heaven on earth.

Then there are the kindergarten ducks.

I have a friend who works with a class of urban preschoolers. Last spring, she thought it would be a great learning experience to hatch a bunch of eggs at Easter.

She got some duck eggs and an incubator, I know not where, and the kids observed the whole hatching phenomenon.

Great concept.

The problem is that baby ducks grow at a furious pace. So, within several weeks my friend had a bunch of quackers that had doubled in size, and the kids had bonded to their duckies. It took a whole morning for their teacher to explain that growing ducks belong on farms and ponds, not in school.

Apparently the school's janitorial staff grew insistent. After a frantic late night call, I agreed to take the kindergarten ducks.

I picked up the gaggle and put them in a cardboard box. All I could see were fluffs of yellow down through the diamond-shaped holes the kids had fashioned to give them breathing space. They quacked every time we came to a stop. Really quacked big time in rush hour traffic out of the city. I tried talking to calm them down, but they preferred a motherly "quack." You get some strange looks at stoplights when other drivers spot you quacking at a cardboard box.

At the farm, a dozen handfuls of quacking fluff waddled dutifully into their pen. I put out their duck food and gave them a vat of water, but that was not enough. These ducklings had been socialized. They wanted to follow me around while I did my chores.

Twelve ducklings do nothing but eat and do what comes naturally. I gave them a little duck house to live in and a plastic swimming pool to play in. All summer long I plucked leafy greens from the garden for them to nibble, and they made a great game out of eating every insect that came their way.

They demanded "quality time," quacking away as though I understood just what they were saying. All of this because from the time they came out of their eggs, they became used to the idea that anything larger than them and roughly shaped like a human being would say "quack, quack, quack" to them and give them food.

They liked to be sprayed with the garden hose. They discovered where the nozzle end of the hose was and if I did not turn it on they would poke it with their orange beaks and quack at me as though I were a bad parent.

Now they are grown ducks. They quack a lot louder, and they do what comes naturally in larger amounts. They ate all of the leftover tomatoes from the garden and then they started gobbling corn.

I am a shepherd, not a duckherd. From my point of view as a farm businesswoman, the only future these fine, well-fed waterfowl had was as duck à l'orange.

Then I got the letter from Haley.

"Dear Farmer," she wrote, "I am in Grade One now. How are the ducks? My favourite was Boinker. He said boink instead of quack."

The letter ended with, "I hope Boinker is happy. I love him. Please give him some lettuce." Attached was a picture that approximated a large child holding out her hand to a small yellow creature wearing orange shoes.

What was I supposed to do? What sort of heartless duck foster mother would fire back a letter saying, "Boinker doesn't boink any more and he should be golden brown after two hours at 350 degrees"?

I went to the duck house and called out, "Boinker, come here!"

All of the ducks waddled happily toward me, and I knew I did not have the heart to pluck one feather from any duck that had been to kindergarten.

Let it not be said that old shepherds cannot learn new tricks. A neighbour who raises waterfowl has advised me on how to winterize my duck house.

I even learned how to tell the difference between boy and girl ducks. You do this by turning the duck upside down and gently poking around. Males, who are called drakes, will ultimately raise their drakehood in a rather flimsy display of masculinity.

Now all four of my drakes have blue bands on their duck ankles, so we do not have to go through that undignified procedure again. In the spring, I will divvy up the girlfriends. Building nest boxes can be a winter project.

Then my teacher friend can fire up the incubator and introduce a new batch of kids to the miracle of life. But those little quackers will not be coming back to my farm. I have that one figured out already.

A young couple down the road have just bought a few acres with a little pond and they want to have some ducklings. They are thrilled that at least one of them might say "Boink."

I wrote back to Haley.

"Boinker is fine. His feathers are white. He has learned how to quack like the other ducks, but he still comes if you call him Boinker. Your love helped make him a fine and happy duck. Thanks for letting me look after him.

PS. How did you know that he was a boy duck?"

Sisterhood Can Be Chaos

WHEN THE SHEEP BEGIN TO HAVE THEIR LAMBS, THE chaos theory of farming kicks in. That is to say that no matter how much experience a shepherd has — no matter how well prepared, or attentive — something unpredictable is bound to happen.

There is the medical kit to think about. All sorts of little things to stock. Mineral oil to remedy constipated lambs and Pepto-Bismal for little fellows with diarrhea. There are plastic paddles with shoe laces tied to them that are intended for use on ewes who suffer from gynaecological prolapses. I tried this out once and immediately called the vet. Still, there they are in the medical kit like a reminder from a David Cronenberg horror film of what happens when things get worse.

I also have a margarine tub filled with Epsom salts to use as a warm wash over tender udders. Sometimes I use it on my own weary fingers when I make a cup of tea in the middle of lambing — dipping my digits in the margarine tub filled with soft warm water with one hand and sipping a cuppa Earl Grey in the other. I have Handi-Wipes, in the kit along with rubbing alcohol, Band-Aids for me, just in case, and iodine to daub on the lambs' umbilical cords to prevent infection.

The kit is stocked with elixirs and medicines that I hardly ever have to use. There are usually a few orange-flavoured cough drops thrown in. I use them on myself or I give them to a ewe who is bored waiting to deliver her lambs.

Diversions are also an important part of birthing.

The sheep all know my little medical kit. Many of them have been butting their heads against it since they were lambs. It is a battered yellow plastic lunch-box type-thing that a child once gave me. On the side of it is the lettering "Dr. U. Be Well."

I carried the kit into the barn last week in the middle of a chill but calm night. It had been four hours since the last barn rounds, and the sandman was still in my eyes. When sheep start to have their lambs, there is no particular time or reason. They do it in the dark, or at dawn or in the middle of Sunday brunch. When one does it, another is sure to follow — or it may be days until a whole slew decide to try for a simul-birthing at supper time.

What I found this night was two sister ewes — Franny and Zooey — in full birthing pre-performance. They are three year olds, both big husky girls with the same long crimp to their wool. If you removed their yellow ear tags, it would be hard to tell them apart without checking their tattoos. They walk alike, they baa alike and they both chew their cud in a clockwise motion. I checked my breeding records and, sure enough, they both had romantic interludes with the ram on the same October day.

It followed that they would both decide to have their lambs in the same corner of the barn at the same time.

Head to head, I found them pawing diligently at the straw, turning in circles to arrive back at the same spot. Fanny was the first one to lie down and begin pushing, arching her head backward to the sky and groaning great sheep groans. All the while her sister pawed at the straw around her and made the same sort of guttural sounds an Inuit throat singer would make if imitating a pregnant sheep.

There was great excitement when a large glob of lamb slid easily from Fanny. Both ewes had licked it clean before I could get anywhere close. That was when I noticed that Zooey was taking a proprietary interest in Franny's baby.

The lamb did not mind the attention at all. In no time, the little guy was on its soft hooves wobbling around and looking for some milk. Franny tried to nose it in her direction, but Zooey was right there as well, offering to feed a newborn that was not hers. Then Franny gave another great groan and sat down like a giant dog. She curled over on her side to give birth to another lamb.

This was just the opportunity Zooey needed. While Franny was busy doing her sheep Lamaze breathing, Zooey was cuddling and cooing over her sister's lamb, fairly inviting the newborn critter to file for adoption papers.

Franny delivered her second lamb without a problem. A fine big ram lamb with a tip of white on the end of his tail. Both ewes were on him like a flash, nuzzling and licking and making quiet eh-eh-eh sounds to let him know that mother was near. Or rather mothers.

I went off to get fresh straw and a portable pen to put them into. By the time I got back Franny and Zooey were contentedly nursing one lamb apiece — as though sharing udders and lambs was a natural act of sisterhood. Zooey seemed to have completely forgotten that she was still in labour. In fact, she seemed relieved to have avoided the whole contraction and pushing routine. Without the pain, she had the gain.

Sisterhood is powerful. When I had the pen set up for Franny and her two lambs, I discovered how powerful it is. I took the lamb Franny was nursing and backed into the pen with it while she followed, baaing with great concern. Once installed, she finally realized that something was missing — her other lamb. Whatever horror a ewe can reflect in her face was written on poor Franny's when she saw her other lamb nuzzling his Aunt Zooey's bountiful udder.

I tried to approach Zooey casually, using a handful of grain to divert her attention from the abduction I was planning.

Scooping the lamb, I made a dash for the pen and plopped it in beside Franny. That is when Zooey butted me a good one in the backside, sending my toque flying into Franny's pen where it landed squarely over the face of the lamb with the white-tipped tail. I leaped into the pen, as much for safety as to retrieve my cap.

Franny did not mind me being there, she busied herself with sniffing both lambs — first one, then the other and back again. Sheep do not count much past two or three.

Outside the pen an irate and frantic Zooey circled like a bull after blood. Long baleful baas whined out of her. She was so caught up she did not even seem to notice that she had passed a water-bag the size of a grapefruit.

Then suddenly she flopped into the straw, arched her nose to the sky and groaned. A few minutes later she had her own lamb to lick and coo over. Then another, and another.

Sisterhood can also be productive.

After a week or so of togetherness, Franny and Zooey and their lambs will be turned in with a pen of lambs and mothers who have bonded with each other sufficiently to know who belongs to whom. With triplets to care for, Zooey is too busy with her own brood to contemplate lamb-napping her sister's twins.

There is nothing in my medical kit that deals with maternal instinct. It cannot be injected, prevented or prompted. It just happens as naturally in a sheep barn as it does in a maternity ward.

I have two more sister sheep who are waiting to have their lambs. But one has big old floppy ears and the other has pointy ears that twitch like propellers. One chews clockwise, the other chews counterclockwise. I do not think they even like each other much.

But if I find them both pawing in the straw together, readying to deliver their lambs at the same time — nothing will surprise me about the chaotic sisterhood of sheep.

The Great Squirrel Diaspora

SQUIRRELS DO NOT ALWAYS LIVE IN TREES. GIVEN HALF a chance they are perfectly happy to live indoors. They tend to prefer heights, however, which makes attics ideal. Once they set up house, it can be very difficult to evict them, and the sound of little feet scampering overhead multiplies awfully quickly.

A plague of red squirrels invaded my friend Barbara's garage. Since the garage is attached to the house, invasion of the attic was imminent. Food sources were battened down. The dog slept in the garage as a warning to fur-bearing rodents. But at night Barbara could hear them scampering along the rooftop, frolicking in the eaves-troughs, looking for any easy access. Soon they were chittering happily somewhere in the attic.

Barbara is a gentle soul. She could not bring herself to poison the squirrels, especially not after finding a nest of hairless ruddy babies squeaking helplessly in a ceiling crawl space. To her, every red squirrel was as endearing as Beatrix Potter's Squirrel Nutkin. She waited until they were big enough to leave the drey — as squirrel nests are called — and then she brought out the humane trap.

One litter of squirrel babies proved to be just the tip of the red-tailed iceberg in the attic. Every day, Barbara would find one or two new squirrels in the trap. To lure them she used everything from peanut butter to marshmallows to pine nuts. Once trapped, they were transferred to a wire pen in the barn where they devoted themselves to trying to escape. When that failed, they decided to propagate.

The harvest of the squirrels went on for weeks. Just when she thought it had to be over, Barbara would hear the sound of little feet racing across the roof in the moonlight. She had a dream about laughing squirrels and woke up wondering if it had been a dream.

Adolescent squirrels joined adult squirrels and aged squirrels in the barn. When Barbara spotted one particularly plump-looking squirrel gathering materials for a nest, she decided enough squirrels was enough. The squirrel pen was loaded into the back of the truck and she drove them two townships away before letting them loose in a field next to a woodlot. Knowing Barbara, she probably left a bag of nuts with them, just to get them started.

"It is over, done. They are gone. They are free at last," she crowed cleverly.

The way of the world and the way of squirrels being what they are, Barbara was not the only person relocating squirrels hither and yon. In fact, the very day Barbara told me about the great squirrel diaspora, another friend called with a squirrelly tale.

This time squirrels had squatted in Brian's granary. They were bold and thieving squirrels. He tried everything from cats to the anti-terrorist tactic of playing Guns N' Roses at full blast. The squirrels were immovable. Even more disturbing, they seemed to thrive on Heavy Metal. So he trapped them.

Then he took them to a woodlot two townships away and let them go.

Next spring I expect that Brian's Axl Rose-loving nutbusters will be knocking about in Barbara's attic, and Barbara's Squirrel Nutkins will be building condominiums in Brian's granary.

So far, I have not experienced the challenges of living with squirrels. I am lucky. I live three townships away from Brian and Barbara.

A Fine Day for Washing Palominos

THE THING ABOUT MUD ON A FARM IS THAT IT DEVOURS the soul. After the dark days of winter, when the sun finally shines for extended periods, if you look down instead of up, much of what you see is mud. People talk about it. Children wear it on their boots and backsides. Trudging through it, animals draw the sound of sucking ooze with each hoof displacement.

Farmers become cranky when they cannot move machinery onto the land and begin their seeding. They end up talking amongst themselves, stewing and chewing and wringing their hats in coffee shops. At home, even the busiest kitchen linoleum pattern cannot hide the dried streaks of mud that inevitably find their way indoors. Dogs smell of barnyard muck. Chickens roost on slim metal gates to avoid the stuff, and cats balance on cedar fencelines like tight-rope walkers to make their way to higher and drier hunting grounds.

In such an environment it is impossible to feel clean, yet cleaning seems to be the response that heals and motivates.

Windows get washed. Porches are swept. Lawnmowers are scrubbed free of last year's dried grass and emollients smoothed over their plastic places creating an illusion of newness. At hardware stores, little metal brushes that can scrape the grease from hidden places in barbecues enjoy brisk sales.

The first warm windy day of spring finds clotheslines fluttering with alternating strands of shorts and halter tops removed from mothballs and snowsuits and long underwear being prepared for mothballs. At the town laundromat, Mennonite men in work boots line up at the industrial-strength washing machines loading horse blankets that have grown stiff with winter sweat and shedding hair. While the mud is upon the land, the ritual rug-beating of spring becomes its panacea.

I have found myself caught up in this phenomenon and I always wonder why hope seems to spring eternal from hot sudsy water and air drying. On the other hand, when you live with mud for about a month out of every year, the idea of paying to attend a spa where dipping in the stuff is *de rigueur* simply does not compute.

Fortunately, sheep stay away from mud. Lambs will not go near the stuff. This is one of the few innate signs of intelligence that sheep display. Horses, on the other hand, do not seem to differentiate between mud, manure and green pastures. They will lie down in anything, which is particularly distressing when they are of a pale hue.

My horses are palominos — "designer equines" some would say. Their bloodlines are a mixture of American Saddlebred, Thoroughbred and Quarter Horse, with a dollop of Arabian in there somewhere to provide a fine perk to their ears and some distance between their dark eyes. A mother and daughter team, they have yet to earn a cent toward their upkeep. I call them riding horses but to anyone wrestling with the red ink of farming they are little more than pasture decorations, otherwise known as "hayburners." Still, old Lady, the mother, and her fully mature daughter, Karma, gladden my heart with their coats of gold fringed with white manes and tails. They are the kind of horses that the good guys got to ride in old Western movies, and the feminist cowperson in me strikes a blow for all women when I put them under saddle and gallop into the sunset.

But mud destroys any mindset of palomino mythology. Spring bedraggles both of them. Their shaggy winter coats come off in handfuls of hairballs, leaving them as patchy shades of yellow mixed with whatever muck they have come up against. So I do the only thing that seems to trigger positive endorphin activity in the mud-swamped brain of spring — I wash them.

There is always one spring day when the temperature soars beyond whatever lie the weekend weather person has perpetrated. It is the day that fragile tomato transplants begin taking firm root. It is the day when the fragrance of lilac blossoms mingles with the smell of cars being waxed. And that makes it a fine day for washing palominos.

You basically wash a horse from the top down. I spray the whole working area and follow that with gobs of livestock shampoo. Lady goes first and Karma follows. Neither one is the least bit reticent, until it comes to spraying their bellies. I dress for the event in tatters of clothes that never need to see mothballs again. Standing on an old fruit box in the sun, rubbing a smelly old horse might not be everyone's ideal of spring cleaning, but it works for me.

Horse washing takes a good half a day. At the end of it, the horses gleam. Tangle-free, platinum blonde manes and tails float with any breeze. Blackened hooves look ready to tap-dance. The horse washer, however, is generally a soggy mess of half-dried lather matted with horse hair.

When the horses are freed in their pasture, it is like a scene from a picture book. They trot smartly with their heads aloft, snorting and flaunting their fair complexions to the whisper of grass. Sometimes their muzzles meet. Then their heads shake away in a flurry of stiff-legged bucking that ends in a canter glide to the far fenceline and back. Pulling up stock-still, they look poised, collected and ready for their close-up.

It is best to leave them in that instant of wonder and beauty. Somewhere in the pasture there is a swale. Lady and Karma know the spot well. To them it is a panacea that oozes an invitation to lie down and roll. Kicking at clouds, they let their souls wallow in the last mud of spring. As rituals go, it must be a lot more fun than rug-beating.

Pavlov's Sheep

FLEXIBILITY IS KEY TO SURVIVING IN THE COUNTRY. Years ago, asthma forced my veterinarian to give up his farm animal clientele, as well as his own flock of sheep. He became a federal meat inspector, with a small practice for dogs and cats on the side just because he loves animals. When his wife Pat and her nurse friend, Jan, opened a specialty butcher shop and delicatessen, Dr. Ron became their part-time butcher and sausage maker. His smoked sausages are the absolute best, and — coincidentally — his partner in sausage making is Jan's husband, Norm, who is a firefighter. It has all evolved quite naturally. However, when you are hosting a barbecue get-together, guests tend to pause when you explain that a vet and a fireman made the smoked sausage that they are so enthusiastic about.

People who start farming from scratch and have a dream that they will make a living at it, have to be flexible enough to appreciate that simply not losing money may be a more realistic goal. Subsidization is often a necessity.

This can take many forms from finding a job in a nearby town, to driving a school bus or inventing a home-based business. If you have a spare room and a decent recipe for muffins, the next thing you know you have a bed and breakfast. Farmers should not have to work double-time to make a living, but we do. When all is said and done, it boils down to the lifestyle.

I know a retired farmer who makes more money playing the pork bellies futures market than he ever did actually raising pork bellies. But he still keeps a miniature Vietnamese pot-bellied pig in the backyard of his tidy house in town. Every spring he "just happens" to stop by my barn to look at the newborn lambs, before he heads off down the road to check on the neighbour's calf crop.

Writing is an easy occupation to combine with farming, although it shares the same sporadic income pattern and rush to deadlines as market gardening and lambing seasons. Also, it has an invisible element. Advances in computer technology and electronic information retrieval allow a writer to function virtually anywhere in the world. Often it is just a question of convincing an editor that an article from a Rural Route address has the same cachet as one that comes from Downtown. In terms of journalism, a telephone interview is a telephone interview, no matter what area code it comes from.

One of the first things I added to my barn was a telephone. While working away — whether collecting eggs, stacking hay or grooming a horse — I leap at the sound of the telephone, bounding over gates and lunging up alley-ways to make the connection.

At first, the sheep ignored this flurry of activity. But

after a month or so, they developed a stomach-centred telephone response. They baa mercilessly when the phone rings.

Sheep are basically stomachs covered with wool. As ruminants, they have four stomachs, each of which seems to need to have something to do. Unless they are sleeping, sheep are constantly engaged in some action related to eating or chewing.

Commands such as "Cease and desist!" or variations thereof have no effect on sheep. To shut them up, I keep a pail of grain beside the phone and toss the contents in their trough before I say "hello."

The effect of this is Pavlovian. Even a wrong number earns the sheep an added treat. Sometimes I have as many as two calls in an hour and I forget to replenish the grain bucket. The second call is always one of some importance.

On one such occasion, an editor of a fledgling fashion magazine was calling. The sheep were relentless and I could not hear a word she was saying. When I called her back from the house, my apologetic explanation seemed to relieve her.

"Oh, I'm glad it was just sheep," she said. "I was afraid you had very unusual children."

Another time, I was desperately trying to get an interview with the chairman of a stock exchange. The story had the scent of scandal, so I was not the only journalist trying to obtain such an interview. While the distinguished gentleman declined my request, the sheep baaed willfully in the background.

"Are those sheep?" I heard him ask, while I strained the phone cord to reach around the corner for a scoop of grain to silence the lot of them.

"Yes, sir," I responded as professionally as a person could while balancing over a grain trough and flinging oats at caterwauling ruminants.

"What kind, might I ask? I grew up on a farm, you know."

While the sheep chewed, we chatted about farm life — his and mine. Gradually we came back to the topic of business, which became an interview.

As it turned out, I got the "scoop" — and so did the sheep.

It's a Wonderful Dog's Life

TRADITIONALLY, FARM DOGS BARK WHEN STRANGERS come up the laneway. The dogs can be any breed, but usually they are a mixture of a few designed to be loyal to their masters. They chase the odd cat or groundhog, but little kids can pull their tails without fear. Farm dogs eat kibble and table scraps. They do not whine, and they only howl when they have a marauding raccoon up a tree. Good sheepherding dogs can work a flock tidily into the barn or shift them from one field to another with a combination of quiet precision and bursts of speed. They work for a living.

I have never had a good sheepherding dog, and the only living my various dogs have made has been the veterinarian's. Still, most of the dogs who have lived on the farm at least bore some farm dog traits.

The Bullmastiff Mingus was the namesake of legendary jazz bass player Charlie Mingus who was as massive as his instrument. Dog Mingus was also massive. From a breadbox of a puppy he grew to develop a head the size of a 4H calf's and the body to go with it. His bark could shake a coon out of a tree.

The Ming was a lovable character. He was the kind of dog who inspired men in groups to offer him a beer. Brave-hearted two year olds thought he was an over-sized stuffed toy to be tweaked and mutilated. And he did tricks. Watching him sit up and beg was akin to watching an elephant rise on its haunches. Hold two fingers in front of his nose and he would bark. The dog snored louder than a tugboat fog horn.

But Mingus was a collar-slipping kind of dog. He took to wandering, and nothing from love to surgery, from discipline to electric fence could stop him. He was going to play with the dog one-tenth his size who lived next door no matter what. I would see him halfway across the field and run at top speed, hurdling the electric fence, to chase him and call him back. He would stop momentarily, shake his great head, spew some muzzle juice and lope off.

When I went to pick him up, I would often find him happily chewing chicken bones that the little dog was allowed to eat. Thus horrified, I would then have to hoist the huge dog one half at a time into the pickup truck. The day he decided to spare me the effort and walk home along the sideroad was the day a cement truck hit him. I still miss everything about him, except his bad breath.

Other dogs have come and gone. Stella, an Akita, who was raised by a hairdresser and lived most of her life on the twenty-eighth floor of an apartment building, never fully adapted to the farm. She would bark at the bird feeder but ignore an oil truck coming up the lane.

Sheltie, a Shetland Sheepdog I adopted from the family of newspaper potentate Conrad Black, spent most of her waking hours barking at anything that moved. Together, they formed one semi-cohesive farm dog. Both dogs lived on the farm until they died and their memory is as bonded to the land as their graves. Still, there is always some psychic gap to raising dogs you did not start with as puppies, some youthful experience unshared that will always remain unknown. Where, for example, did Stella develop a fear of hockey pucks? Why did Sheltie like to urinate in men's shoes?

My next dog was going to be a puppy. I discounted the possibility of ever having a dog that did a day of work in its life, so I deliberately sought out a breed that interested me from an aesthetic point of view. I chose a knee-high wrinkly breed, a relatively rare breed and an offensively over-priced canine: the Chinese Shar Pei. At the breeder's, the puppy came close to picking herself out of the litter by tumbling out of a squirming pile of wrinkled siblings to have a look at me. She licked my ankles. Her tongue matched the colour of her coat — jet black.

Diva Dog's name sprang automatically, since she was a born prima donna with a faultlessly assured attitude. Her wrinkles made her a daily photo opportunity, but gradually she grew to fit her skin. With the exception of her ears and a few lines on her forehead, the final dog emerged as a compaction of solid muscle.

"Kinda dog is that?" farmers would ask. "Looks like a pit bull with a pig's tail."

A long-winded explanation would follow, delineating the distinctions between Shar Peis and pit bulls and

Staffordshire Bull Terriers and any other breed. Finally, I gave up trying to make a case for a wrinkle dog that had no wrinkles.

"Marsha ironed her when she was little," became Moose's stock response. End of story.

Diva's bark is appropriate and loud. She chases groundhogs with a passion and digs so far into their holes that I think she might well end up back in China. Early on, when a nesting goose grabbed her loose puppy skin, she learned to give a wide berth to anything wearing feathers. After almost a decade, she still twirls like a top and spins ludicrously around the yard. Among her tricks is the art of lying perfectly still and, instead of shaking paws, she gives "five," slapping her catlike paw across my palm. Overall, she is one of the happiest animals I have ever known.

It is her relationship with lambs that is most curious. During lambing time, Diva will not leave the barn. From outside the pen, she watches constantly. Baby lambs who toddle near the fence are greeted with loving licks.

One morning I arrived at the barn to find two newborn lambs already dried and suckling. While I cursed myself for not being there sooner, Diva bounced frantically outside of the pen. When all was fed and done and I tried to leave the barn, the dog circled around me in ever tightening circles, herding me back.

Then I heard a sleepy little baa. Tucked next to a feeder almost out of sight, there was a triplet lamb, probably the first born and the first to eat. He was just waking up after that first snooze of life with a full tummy and a warm place to sleep. With two lambs demanding her attention, the ewe had apparently forgotten about this self-sufficient fellow.

I let Diva into the pen and she ran to the lamb. While I got the iodine for its navel, Diva fussed with the lamb, nudging him to his feet just like a miniature, mothering ewe. When we presented the foundling to its mother, she stamped her hooves at Diva with as much physical anger as a sheep can muster and took over. I closed the gate and the dog whined. Not a sheepdog, perhaps, but certainly a friend of sheep.

A traditional farm dog Diva will never be. She is unlikely to learn that I am not thrilled by the gift of a dead skunk on the front lawn. Nor do I appreciate spending Sunday afternoon at the vet's office while porcupine quills are wrested from her muzzle. But when she lays with her back legs splayed and her head flattened against the grass, snoozing beside the lilies-of-the valley and barking at her dreams, it's a wonderful dog's life.

Letting the Air Out

As AN URBANITE, ALL I KNEW ABOUT CHICKENS WAS
that I liked to eat them and they were a source of eggs.
Much has been learned about the vagaries, species and
confounding behaviours of poultry since then, but for me
it all started with the "capon."

For years, I had seen the word "capon" used in fancy
restaurants where it appeared as a high-priced "breast of"
item — usually roasted or grilled — and always "succu-
lent." At city supermarkets, the capon in the poultry section was presented as a meaty chunk of a bird, slightly
smaller than a turkey, but always a chunk of change more
than common chicken. Add the words "free range" to
capon and the price went even higher. Since my farm
seemed to be nothing but free-ranging space, I figured I
could make a killing growing capons for my city friends.

Sometime in March, I picked up the list of what sort of
chicks were available at the local Co-Op farm supply store.
All manner of fowl were itemized — everything from
goslings to pheasants. At the bottom of the list, there were

capons. They were more expensive, but then by the time they were delivered they would be three weeks old, as opposed to the day-old varieties of most other chicks. Since all of my chicken books said that mortality would be highest in the first few weeks of chick-raising, I figured the added price of buying fully started capons would be worth it. I ordered fifty capons. The hatchery was notified.

By the time "Chick Day" came, I had everything set up according to the book. Heat lamps were strategically placed above the wood shavings in a well-ventilated pen that I had personally disinfected. The chick waterers were slightly raised so that the chicks could not foul them with their fowl droppings. There were long rows of aluminum feeders specially designed to allow only the chicks' heads to get at the food. I even installed a paper towel rack beside the doorway to the pen, lest I need to wipe anything untoward from my hands.

Chick Day turned out to be a noisy affair. Lining the store alleyways there were corrugated boxes full of peeping, chirping and squawking new life forms. Four boxes had my name on them.

One by one, I unloaded the capons at the barn. They were bigger than the day-old chicks that were on display beside the coffee machine at the Co-Op, but they still had a lot of growing to do. I dunked each tiny yellow beak into the water so that they got the idea right from the start.

Within a few hours they had fed and watered themselves, soiled their fresh wood shavings and settled down to sleep under their cosy heat lamps. I breathed a sigh of relief and went to bed.

The next morning I hurried to the chick pen to see

how my partially feathered charges had managed the night. Some were startled to see me scooping food into their troughs, others looked up and ran around in circles. A few just lay there like cantaloupes on the vine.

They looked like cantaloupes, too. While the others were taut packages of feathered wings and downy under-bellies, the cantaloupe capons were positively bloated. I knew they were supposed to grow quickly, but this was ridiculous. I picked one up and it felt like yesterday's balloon from a bridal shower. I ran for the phone.

"They're blowing up," the woman at the hatchery told me. "You've got to let the air out."

"Hello," I said, holding the phone in one hand, examining the chick in my other hand as though it was a live grenade. "What do you mean 'blowing up'?"

Patiently, the voice on the other end of the line explained that capons are just male chickens, simple roosters, that have gone through a small surgical process that removes or prevents the manufacture of testosterone. Thus the "caponized" bird grows to adulthood with the frame of a male and the breast meat of a female. In the meantime, air is sometimes drawn into the surgical site, causing the birds to "puff up."

I was told to take a sterilized hypodermic needle and re-puncture the small healing scar area that I would find on the underside of each afflicted chick. This was to be followed by squeezing.

"You just squeeze until you've let the air out," the hatchery woman said, as casually as though she was telling me to pour salt on a red wine stain and then vacuum.

"Excuse me," I exhaled.

"Well you don't want them to blow up, do you?" came the response.

At this point, I was too early in my career as a farmer to have learned anything about giving animals injections. And I had no idea where I was going to purchase a hypodermic needle in a small rural town without being labelled a junkie.

I called my doctor's office and asked the receptionist to have him call me as soon as possible on an urgent matter of an extremely personal nature involving life or death. He called right away.

"Tom," I whispered into the receiver, "I need a hypodermic needle or my chickens will blow up."

Dr. Tom is a man known for his calm and kindly bedside manner. Even in a crisis situation, his demeanour is such that you have the feeling that just touching the sleeve of his white gown will make everything all right.

"Tell me about it from the beginning," he said.

When I was done, I imagined him holding his head at his desk and chastising himself for not detecting this obvious insanity during a routine check-up.

"Look Marsha," he said. "Just go into the store where you got the chickens and ask them for what you need. It is perfectly legal, trust me. Sterilize the needle with alcohol each time, and make as small an entry as possible without probing into the muscle tissue. Call me if you have any problems."

Okeedokie, I said to myself, and I headed for town.

As casually as possible, I approached the counter where a young fellow with the body structure of a Hereford calf was serving customers.

"I would like a hypodermic needle," I announced.

"You want disposables? What gauge? And do you need a syringe?" he asked as though selling hypodermics was an everyday occurrence.

"Disposables are fine," I blurted. "Small, very small."

"Well, is it for a calf or a pig, or what?" he asked.

By this time our conversation had attracted the attention of waiting customers. I leaned across the counter and quietly said, "It's for my capons. They're blowing up."

Even the stoic Mennonite farmer standing behind me burst out laughing. Red-faced, I left the store with a little brown bag and complete instructions on assembling the device.

Back at the barn, a couple of the chicks had expanded to near volleyball size. I laid out my tools on an upturned grain bucket, wondering all the while what St. Augustine, the patron saint of animals, would have to say about this schmozzle.

The first one was the scariest. I propped the little fellow on his back against a towel and looked for the troublesome scab site. Then ever so gently I nudged the tip of the needle into the little brown scab.

Nothing happened. There was no sound. The bird did not flinch. I do not know what I was expecting, but this sure was not it.

I picked up the little capon and cradled both puffy sides of him, squeezing him softly with my eyes closed tight. Then I felt a slight breeze on my cheek.

It was working! A slow but steady stream of air was flowing from the tiny hole. My capon was deflating.

It took about five minutes to let all of the air out. I

completed the job by spraying the wound site with Bactine and releasing the "patient." He cocked his head and casually trotted off to the feed trough.

I let the air out of a dozen capons that day. All of them lived.

When I was ready to market the capons, customers lined up for the androgynous birds. In accordance with their dubious beginnings, I sold each capon at an inflated price.

Mother's Day in Bloom

I GROW A HILLSIDE FULL OF DAFFODILS FOR MOTHER'S Day — but my Mother never gets them — someone else's mother does.

It all started about fifteen years ago when I temporarily lost fiscal sanity and bought a couple of hundred daffodil bulbs. One brisk fall day, I planted every last one of them on a hillside next to the forest, just beside the roadway at the end of the farm lane.

Visions of a miniature rolling meadow dotted with nodding trumpet heads of yellow filled me with anticipation all that winter. And, when the daffodils made their debut the following May, it made any memory of muddy April disappear. Every time I turned the truck up the lane it made me smile.

Over the next five years, I added clumps of lilies, tall poppies and iris to the hillside. Any flowering perennial that could be divided and transplanted from the garden beds around the farm house ended up finding a place on the hill. Some thrived, some faded away. Wild flowers added their own colour.

Every spring the daffodils grew in number. Left to their own devices they divided and conquered like a Dutch army. On Mother's Day, I had a big vase filled with daffodils in the house and when my Mother visited, she could leave with an armload of yellow flowers that we plucked from the wayside garden.

But about a decade ago something changed. When I went down the lane to pick the Mother's Day daffodils, they were gone. Every bloom had disappeared, leaving only the unfolded buds to provide a smattering of what once was, when they flowered a few days later. The hillside had been plucked like a chicken.

I was angry. I felt robbed and personally denuded. But there was nothing at all to be done. I still had batches of daffodils around the house. That was not the point. The flowering hillside had been a fantasy. To me it was like something out of A.A. Milne's Winnie the Pooh and Christopher Robin stories — "a warm and sunny spot" in the landscape; "that enchanted place on the top of the forest where a little boy and a bear will always be playing."

Then some ignoramus wrecked it all, on Mother's Day to boot.

Since then the Mother's Day flower theft has become an annual event.

One year, I put out a "no trespassing" sign, but the wind blew it over and it looked fairly silly and mean-spirited to begin with.

My neighbours began noticing that the hillside of yellow joy only survived for a few days every spring. Some of them had their own fantasy of me living in a house filled with daffodils in vases in every room. When I told them the terrible truth, they started keeping watch over the roadway around Mother's Day, but no one ever saw the blooming bandit.

Suggestions poured in to accompany the solutions that fermented in my own fevered brain.

Leghold traps were out of the question, because small forest animals and deer sometimes crossed the hillside. Electric fencing would have been a nice solution, except it is far too visible to any daytime daffodil stalker, and you cannot clear-cut an entire hillside in the dark.

An older gentleman suggested incarcerating a pen of geese on the hillside to act as an early warning defence system. It seemed like a good idea, except all of my geese were sitting on eggs.

The one big goose I did manage to install in a makeshift chicken wire pen halfway down the laneway honked and screamed all night long. By dawn, he had beaten his way out of the pen with his powerful wings. That failure was heard all along the concession.

Someone suggested I try camping in the forest behind the hill overnight and catching the culprit yellow-handed. I even had the offer of a paint gun — the sort that crazed mercenary wannabes play with as a splatter game sport. But I am not the sort who can curl up grace-fully in a pup tent and sleeping bag when I have a com-fortable bed within striking distance. And I just could not imagine myself rising from the hillside like a sleepy G.I. Jane and launching a missile of red paint on a crouched daffodil thief at dawn. I could, however, imag-ine missing my target and ending up with a hillside cov-ered in red paint.

A child came up with the most inventive, non-combative solution. She suggested that I find a baby skunk to be a pet and keep it at a special skunkhouse on the hillside. Then the skunk could stink up any intruder and the flowers would live happily ever after. It was a charming idea, but I have never found a skunk to be that friendly. Better a hillside without flowers than a hillside filled with stink blossoms.

So I have resigned myself to enjoying the daffodils while they sway, oh so briefly, on the hillside. Five years ago, I began digging up bulbs and separating them, taking a few back to the farmhouse every year and planting them in the fenced orchard meadow just outside the kitchen.

Now it does not bother me when the daffodils disappear. I turn the truck up the lane on Mother's Day and sigh. But somewhere I imagine that there is a mother who is blessed with a bigger vase of flowers than she had ever hoped for. If she is a good mother, someday she will discover the personality defect in the off-centre offspring who gives her an ill-gotten gift and she will correct it.

In the meantime, there are plenty of daffodils in the orchard field for my Mother and I to pluck on Mother's Day, or any other May day that happens along.

And in the end, that is what it is all about.

Being with Mother.

Leaping Lizards,
It's Jumping Sheep

SHEEP ARE NATURAL BORN JUMPERS. LIKE IAN MILLAR and Big Ben, they soar over obstacles with a rectitude that can be breathtaking.

Sometimes I think sheep jumping should be an Olympic event. Our great Canadian jumping sheep would have a terrific advantage over the free-ranging Australian sheep who barely ever see a fence. Of course, we would have to watch out for the British jumping sheep. Goodness knows, they might find the genetic marker for jumping over tall buildings in a single bound and clone a whole team of high-flying Dollys.

I am not kidding when I say that sheep can really jump. By the time they are three months old most lambs could easily clear the heads of most five year olds. It is only up from there.

And they don't just jump. They spring, almost as though they have rubber bands in their knees. It actually begins when lambs are two or three days old. Wobbly woollen bundles start bobbing around their mothers like pop-up pool balls on the ricochet. They do this for no apparent reason other than the sheer joy of it.

When they are grown, jumping sheep are a problem. Sometimes the only way to contain them in their field is with a strand or two of electric fencing. A tingle of that on their tummies as they ease over a fence is a sure cure. Even in winter, when the electric fence is turned off, sheep maintain a healthy respect for it. They do not know it is unplugged.

This year, however, my electrified strand took a beating. I discovered one whole section of it coiled and crumpled near the barn. For all I know it could have been dragged there by a low-flying goose.

I kept intending to restring the ruse, but other springtime chores got in the way and most of the ewes were either giving birth in the barn or too pregnant to jump anyway.

This leaves the ram. And the ram loves to jump. He jumps without fear, and he jumps without reason — which is one of the reasons that he is called Rambo. Once he jumped off a storey-high wagon of hay in a spine-tingling display of stupidity. Instead of ending up squashed in the yard, he landed upright, gave himself a shake and jumped the fence back into the field.

So when old Rambo finally noticed that there was no voltage impediment to jumping over one section of the fence, he just had to try it. I discovered this one morning when I opened the front door to let the dog out. There was the ram, calmly grazing on sunflower seeds that he had knocked out of the front porch bird feeder.

Well, I would have none of that. I dashed for my

boots and the only tool I thought suitable — my broom. Thus armed, I attempted to bully Rambo off the porch. I poked him. I called him names that would make Sylvester Stallone himself blush. Then I tried irritating him into compliance. I swept his nose.

But those sunflower seeds had an irresistible allure. When he finally finished eating them, the ram looked up at me as though asking for seconds.

So I gave him a whack on the rump, solid enough that it would penetrate through his winter wool. Then I stood down on the steps and waited for him to take me seriously.

Inspired, or perhaps just stunned by my unshepherdly violence, the ram drew himself to his full and noble height. Next thing I knew, he was headed for me. Barrelhousing across the porch with his head down, he threw himself across the steps. With both hands, I raised the broom defensively in front of me.

The last thing I heard was the crack of the broom handle breaking.

Rambo struck me with full force. I came to in a puddle of wet grass about six feet from where I had been standing, still clutching the remnants of my broom. My eyeglasses were neatly scattered around me — in four pieces.

Bruised, blurry-eyed, and feeling more than a tad vanquished, I crawled back to the porch. The ram was nowhere to be seen. I finally found him in the backyard where he was butting at another bird feeder and nibbling on fallen niger seed. When that was gone, he did the logical thing and jumped back into the field. But I knew he would be back.

That afternoon, I spent an hour or so rewiring my

fenceline. The sheep gave passing notice to my labours. Only the horses seem to marvel at the fact that I can touch materials that otherwise electrify them.

In the barn, the spring lambs bounce around as though they are tethered to bungy cords. Their ears flop and their tails jiggle when they hit the ground. They butt their heads together and then jump backwards. They fly through the air and kick up their heels.

It is all quite endearing, but one day they will be full-blown jumping sheep.

After all, they are their father's children.

The Barn Duck in Lust

*I*T IS SPRING AND THE BARN DUCK IS IN LOVE. IT IS NOT A seasoned, mature love, but rather the unchained lust of a duck that does not know he is a duck. The barn duck is in love with a barred rock hen, but I fear his passion will be unrequited, because the old hen has been around the barn long enough to know that she is not a duck.

The barn duck is an odd one. I call him Groucho, because he runs slouched forward, with his wings folded tight and his little orange feet going a mile a minute. Although he is primarily black, a few arches of white above his eyes give him the look of the infamous Marx Brother and I could well imagine a cartoonist drawing him with one of Groucho's trademark cigars.

Much smaller than the big white Emden ducks and the gentle Mallards, he also walks upright like a penguin — or a man for that matter. Although he has wings, he cannot fly. He just runs faster than anything on two webbed feet.

Groucho is an Indian Runner duck. I hatched him

two years ago. In fact, he was forming in the incubator when a fox killed his parents and all of his kin.

Indian Runners are a helpless kind of duck. I have seen geese actually face off with a fox, waving their strong wings fearlessly and wagging their ugly spiked goose-tongues. Even fat geese and ducks can usually raise themselves into the air long enough to find some safety. But Indian Runners can only run; otherwise they are quite literally, sitting ducks.

In fact, I acquired my original gang of Indian Runners because they run. My neighbours, Scotty and Sarah McComb, raise all sorts of fowl, but they never eat them. Their birds are destined for the show ring or other fowl-fanciers' farms. When Scotty showed me their big flock of Indian Runners, a huge grin swept his face.

"Useless as sticks," he laughed. "But just watch them run."

Sure enough he rattled his grain pail and hollered "Here Duck, Here Duck," and the whole colourful lot of them came quacking over the hill into the yard. Running like upright maniacs.

There is something absurdly joyful about running ducks. That is what Scotty said he liked about them. And so did I, until the fox came and started plucking them one by one. The ducks that ran like men could not outrun a fox. They were not happy when I penned them up, but even then, the fox found a way.

When little Groucho hatched, I vowed that he would always stay within my sight, or within the barn.

Because he is singularly odd, Groucho cannot stay in the same pen as the other ducks. They pick on him, probably as much for his irritating quack as for his differences.

I figure he is better off loose in the barn, where he can roam freely and accompany me as I do my chores, quacking at will when the barn door closes.

Consequently, the only other birds Groucho sees are Guinea fowl and chickens. For the longest time, he hung out with a black and white Polish rooster. Polish chickens are another thing I have collected simply because of their looks. They have huge tufts of feathers on their heads, like great fluffy crowns. My Polish rooster's head is so fine and full that the feathers sometimes obliterate his vision, which may be the reason that he accepted Groucho as his buddy. At night they sleep together, the Indian Runner duck and his visually challenged Polish friend.

Groucho's love affair with the barred rock hen started a few weeks ago. She was quietly sitting on her nest making the clucking sounds that go with producing an egg. I watched the little duck scramble up on a bale of hay beside her. He looked down at the hen, quacked furiously and pounced. Apparently ducks do not believe in foreplay.

The hen was beside herself. Before this, she had simply ignored the duck the way all of the chickens did. Now he was astride her trying to grab the back of her neck with his tough duck beak — and she was in the middle of passing an egg.

This breach of etiquette did not elude the Polish rooster, who heard the commotion and tried to figure out where it was coming from. Before he could scoot the feathers from his eyes, three other hens were pecking away at Groucho. The duck finally surrendered to their will.

Now I have to watch Groucho every day. When I start doing chores, he waddles at my feet, quacking at lambs and just quacking in general. As we get close to the chicken pen, he starts stomping his little webbed feet. Weaving back and forth, anxiously.

I have to be quick. If the pen door stays open one second too long, the duck runs straight past me into what he perceives is his personal harem. The mere sight of the lusty duck sends the chickens flying for the rafters, clucking and letting out long chicken growls.

Groucho just stands there. A duck at centre stage. Looking up, flapping his useless wings and quacking.

One of these days — soon — I will have to head over to Scotty and Sarah's and find Groucho a suitable mate. I can put up with another barn duck. The chickens will be pleased to go back to laying their eggs in peace. And maybe Groucho will not be so grouchy if he finds a true love who walks upright and loves to run, and looks a lot like him.

Summer

My Grandmother's House

When I was a kid I used to go to my Grandmother's house, just outside of Stratford, Ontario, in a village called Staffa that consisted of the joining of two roads where there was a General Store and a Post Office.

My Grandmother lived down the road, and most of her children, my aunts and uncles, lived or farmed nearby. The cousins who taught me how to swing on a rope over the haymow still live there.

Many of my fondest childhood memories are set in my Grandmother's house. It was a big, old, two-storey, wood frame house with a cement porch overlooking the front lawn right next to the well pump where Grandmother would crank out her daily water. This was almost forty years ago and the idea that water came out of the ground instead of a tap was fascinating to a kid like me who grew up in the suburbs.

The outhouse was another mystery. It always seemed to take forever to get to the little shed that had two adult-sized apertures and one little hole for kid-sized bottoms.

There was a well-worn path through the raspberry bushes, and once you got there, you stayed until you were done your business even if it meant reading the linen ads in the Eaton's catalogue. The outhouse excursion was my first lesson in planning a daily schedule.

Grandmother's house was basically her kitchen. The other rooms were barely used, or bed chambers. After church, the aunts and uncles and cousins might spill over into the parlour and sit on the good velvet sofa and big stuffed chairs, but the heart of the house was the kitchen.

Everyone would crowd around the kitchen table and talk, while Grandmother quietly went about the business of making pies and cookies and bread. You would rarely see Grandmother without a rolling pin in her hand, or a vegetable peeler, or a boning knife. And she always wore an apron with big pockets that seemed to hold endless supplies of jujubes for us kids.

The meals we had at Grandmother's house were major affairs — meat-and-potato-eating at its most gargantuan. The aunts would arrive with salads. Big leafy green salads, tart spicy bean salads, and impossibly colourful Jello salads that trapped everything from shredded carrots to pineapple and marshmallows in huge molds.

Everything was organic in those days. None of us even knew what a chemical additive was.

While Grandmother supervised the slicing, dicing, boiling and mashing, the uncles would teach the cousins how to play baseball, or show us where to look for turtles and frogs in the pond across the road. By the time it came to actually eating the supper, I remember being almost too tired to chew. No one ever left Grandmother's table hungry, and there was rarely even a wedge of pie left over.

There was always something to do at Grandmother's. Everything from crokinole to cribbage and croquet. Long after we kids had been banished to our quilt-covered beds we would hear whoops of laughter from the kitchen where the adults were playing games of Euchre, Crazy Eights and Hearts. The sound wafted to the second storey through strategically placed holes in the floor that were covered with perforated metal grates that allowed the heat from the wood stove below to rise into the bedrooms. "Listening holes," we called them, and more than once Grandmother's broom handle would poke against the metal advising us nosey children to mind our own business.

You could not sneak around Grandmother's house, because everywhere you went there was some creaking floorboard that would give you away. And once you were in bed, there was no foraging through the raspberry patch to the outhouse. There were "thunder mugs" under the beds to take care of eventualities that could not wait until morning. Even when Grandmother finally got an indoor toilet, we kids would always check under the bed for the thunder mugs, just in case.

You did not loiter in Grandmother's house. You could read a book. You could try to figure out how to make a cat's cradle with your yo-yo. But if you decided to hang out on the sofa in the kitchen doing nothing, Grandmother would scoot you outside "to get the stink blown off."

The same thing would happen to older cousins when they were caught listening in on the telephone party line. I think Grandmother's ring was two long and two short, but it didn't much matter what the ring was if the older cousins were there. They would just quietly pick up and listen to whatever real life neighbourhood soap opera was burning up the lines. Heck, they would even listen to someone else's grocery list — until their cantankerous Grandmother got a hold of their ear, that is.

Grandmother believed in privacy and good manners and order. It was a rare day when even a wisp of her long hair escaped from her hair net, and no child ever left her table without asking to be excused.

Today, all that remains of my Grandmother and her house are old photographs, artifacts and genetics. But memories of her strike me constantly.

If I could relive just one moment in that creaking wooden house that filled with light and love every time some family member slammed the old screen door behind them, it would be one specific wet summer afternoon. Rain pelted down on the old shingled roof and Grandmother sent my father and the grown boys to the dark, dank attic to catch any leaks with pails and thunder mugs.

My mother, and her mother and little me stood at the kitchen door watching the rain bounce off the fresh-cut grass.

"Go on and do it then, Margaret, I know you want to," said my Grandmother to my mother. "And take her with you," she added, meaning me.

Next thing I knew, my mother, MY MOTHER, was stripping off her clothes and Grandmother was telling me to do the same thing.

The screen door opened and out we ran. Leaping over the croquet hoops while the warm rain drenched us, we ran around the yard like naked dervishes.

I will always remember looking back at the doorway of the old house and seeing my Grandmother in her familiar apron. I could hear her laughing, and my mother laughing in the same voice. My own laughing became a part of theirs. I might have been five or six, but I knew that in that one wet and wild moment, we were having the time of our life.

Nothing again will ever be like the times in Grandmother's house. But every time I smell vanilla, I think of Grandmother Fitzgerald because she used to daub it behind her ears as perfume. When I see an old well pump, I can hear the creak hers would make in the morning when the washing-up water was set out. Hollyhocks, delphiniums and climbing roses where the first perennials I planted at my own farm, because I wanted to look out of my kitchen window and see the same riot of colours that sparkled in my Grandmother's eyes.

I think I was about eight years old when I realized, for the first time, that my Grandmother's face had wrinkles. Until then she never seemed to change.

There are many lines from Shakespeare that strike a common chord in all of us. I think of the comic Nurse in *Romeo and Juliet* who notes, "With mirth and laughter let old wrinkles come."

In Grandmother's house, there was always laughter.

Poor Little Lambs
Who Have Gone Astray

*Y*OU CAN GET LOST IN THE COUNTRY. ONE DUSTY sideroad is easy to confuse with another dusty sideroad. If you are finding your way for the first time, some fool is sure to give you directions that say "turn right at the red barn" and, sure enough, every corner you come to has a red barn on it.

Sheep, on the other hand, do not get lost no matter where they wander. They are not born with a compass rose etched in their brains, and there is no one genius sheep in the flock that knows all, sees all and finds all. Sheep navigation is more sensory than scientific. They smell their way home.

Between the toes of every sheep's cloven hooves, there is a nubbly little nodule that excretes a waxy substance. In technical shepherdese, it is called the foot gland.

You would never see it unless you knew what to look for, and sheep do not tend to stand quietly and allow you to pick up their feet as a well-trained horse should. But that little nodule prevents the sheep from forgetting where it lives.

As the sheep stroll through the meadows, the reflex action of walking or gambolling or trotting along renders the scent. Little lost sheep can follow it home like lucky Hansel and Gretels. Once enough sheep follow the same path they stick to it. So it is that all summer long I watch the sheep wander off to their pasture along the same route and return each night the same way.

What I had not known one particular summer was that they had been wandering a longer path than the one in their enclosed pasture for several weeks. They had become rural explorers.

Every morning I innocently opened the gate and watched them amble off for a day of dining from the land. Like clockwork, when the sun was set low in the afternoon sky, they would trundle happily back to the barnyard, skipping along in single file like happy kids getting off the school bus. All seemed right with the world.

Then the policeman came to the door.

He was a bright, shiny young man, but I immediately began feeling guilty of something.

"Do you know anyone around here who has sheep?" he asked.

It seemed an easy enough thing to confess to, but I wanted to test the waters of justice.

"You mean white ones with black heads?" I asked.

"That's them," he said.

My fevered brain began to broil with visions of sheep rustlers, or escaped circus animals feeding on helpless woolly creatures or known bank robbers escaping in sheep clothing.

"Saw them in a field up the road and it doesn't have

any fences, so I thought they might be lost or something," the young officer offered.

I felt better and worse simultaneously. Thanking him for his concern, I prepared to round-up my wayward flock before he called in the paddy wagon.

There is nothing my old horse Lady likes better than asserting her authority over sheep. We cantered into the neighbour's field where the sheep were casually grazing on the leftovers of a harvested barley crop. When the horse stopped, she snorted at them.

All their little black heads turned to look at us. Not an innocent face in the lot. I might as well have caught them smoking cigarettes behind the barn.

Lady started to dance in excitement. She got about three high-stepping prances in before the sheep turned and fled.

They all ran through the same little trampled area in a thicket between two old apple trees. Lady and I kept our distance as the flock settled into a slow jog back along the same route they had come.

If they had been cattle, they might have strayed from the beaten path. That is why we have expressions like, "You could wait till the cows come home." Sheep on the other hand "follow like sheep," and they followed their own footsteps with the same unwavering confidence that robins show when they fly off to Costa Rica for the winter.

At the fenceline, old ewes and young lined up smartly to take turns jumping over a section of cedar rail fence that had collapsed under the weight of a fallen tree branch. It was not their fault that a window opened on a whole new universe.

When they were all safely in the barnyard, I gave them a serious talking to. Haranguing sheep is about as effective as lecturing a Teflon frying pan. Nothing sticks and nothing is absorbed.

Once the fence was repaired, the walk-about sheep contented themselves with strolls through a new gate into fresh pasture. Every evening they dutifully returned, following their scented trail and taking a routine right turn at the red barn.

It is a small comfort to know that while you and I can get lost in the country, ewes can always find their way home.

The Emily Fish

SHORTLY AFTER THE LONGEST DAY OF THE YEAR, THE bass fishing season opens and I can catch Emily again.

Emily is a small-mouthed bass, or a "smallie" as we accomplished bass fisherpeople would say. She lives in a nearby river, in the shadow of a towering concrete bridge connected to a gravel road that hardly anyone uses. It must have cost a million dollars to build that bridge and I cannot help but feel that it was tax dollars well spent if it protects Emily. The sheer magnitude of the bridge and the steep drop below it is enough to dissuade all but the most intrepid intruder.

When I was a kid, fishing meant taking a spool of cotton thread and a safety pin bent at an angle to a sliver of a creek that passed through a cow pasture across from my Grandmother's house. Cousin Elgin would come with me, but only if I dug the worms. We would sit on a makeshift wooden bridge a few feet above the little ripple in the stream and I would wrestle the worms out of the coffee can. Sometimes we dropped a few over the edge to wake the fish up.

Although I was the kind of kid who cried if anyone so much as tried to disfigure my Mr. Potato Head doll, putting a worm on a hook did not faze me. Elgin and I would lower our tortured charges into the water slowly. Then we would watch as little minnows swarmed around, grabbing at bits until there was nothing left. We never did catch a fish in that stream, but we fed a whole lot of them.

After that, I forgot about fishing for several decades, until the Moose decided that he would fish. This resulted in the determination that we would fish. It has become a passion. We fish together, or we fish alone. We have fished all over the world, from jungle rivers in Central America to the great expanses of Georgian Bay. Salted or fresh, if it is wet it is one big fishing hole to me. But country folk hold their fishing holes as close to them as they do their poker hands, so when I found the spot under the bridge, I did not tell so much as one ewe.

This makes catching Emily a secret ritual. When bass season opens, an ultra-light spinning rod is rigged with two-pound test line. I have gone beyond the worms of my childhood, having graduated to plastic cases filled with rubbery jigs in colours that would define a rainbow. Emily prefers yellow. Before I make my cast I squeeze the barb on the hook into oblivion with pliers so it will be easy to let Emily go once she is caught.

The she-bass lies in the deepest part of a pool at the river's edge. While I stand amid the wild iris and shoulder-high grasses, a muskrat sometimes swims across nonchalantly. The sound is of the river and the plopping frogs.

It might take half a dozen casts before Emily rises in a burst. Small-mouthed bass are fighters and she is like a

Ninja acrobat. I have seen her leap straight out of the water and soar before flipping backwards and diving deep. Light line sings off the reel. She leaps again, shaking her fishy head. We battle this way through at least three mosquito bites. Then she either escapes or I bring her to the river's edge, cradle her in the flow of the stream and watch her disappear with a tail flash.

I would never eat her. I would never stuff her and put her on a wall. If the river ever flooded, I would look for her. But I would never tell anyone if I found her, or where. That is a sacred vow I made when I named her.

The first time the fish thrilled me with her power and feist, I heard a voice behind me calling, "Emily, Emily." A rather large man appeared through the underbrush just as she was returning to her pool.

"Name's Brain," he said, brandishing a friendly hand for the shaking. "You know, like in your head. I'm looking for my cat, brown cat, name of Emily."

"Haven't seen any cats," I told him, wondering what kind of man looks for cats beside a difficult stretch of river.

"She's probably home by now anyway. Comes down to the river to watch frogs, I think. Me, I fish," he said.

Then he asked, "You any good at fishing?"

"I couldn't catch a minnow with a worm if I tried," I told him.

"Yeah, I didn't think there'd be many fish in this part of the river," Mr. Brain said as we walked back toward the bridge.

Emily Fish is safe with me.

The Littlest Shearer

*I*N THE WORLD OF SHEEP, SHEARERS ARE A UNIVERSE UNTO themselves. Usually they are shepherds, who strip the wool off other people's flocks to generate a second income. Good shearers are like good plumbers. You book well in advance and give them anything they want when they arrive.

Over the years I have had a number of shearers. Irascible might be the best description. But holding down 250-pound rams and bucking ewes carrying twins while flies hum around and novice shepherds ask dopey questions could make anyone irritable.

Women shearers are at a premium in the rarefied environment of sheep shearers. When I found my shearer, Judy, I felt simpatico, and so did my sheep. She has been shearing the flock ever since. We have sheared with helpers and sheared alone; sheared when we were both having life crises; and sheared when life was perfect. Sometimes there are more sheep, sometimes there are fewer. The one consistent factor is that I collect the dung tags.

Judy was single when we first met. Now she is married

and starting to raise a flock of her own. Nicole was born three years ago. Judy was shearing almost up to her due date. Nicki did not change her mother's schedule much. The sound of clippers and the baa of sheep became the baby's lullabies.

At a year old, Nicole watched the shearing from her car seat set on a bale of straw. At two, she stood on the bale, sucking back bottles of juice and pointing her father Steve in the direction of the next sheep she wanted to see sheared. "Get that ewe, Dad," and he did.

At three, she is truly following in her mother's hoofsteps.

"Your sheep should be dry," she said when she disembarked from the shearing truck in the summer. "Can't shear wet sheep." Her phrasing was exactly as her mother's had been in April.

Cowed by a kid, I assured her that after a wet spring and several missed shearing dates, my sheep were finally dry.

Small and big-eyed, Nicki sat next to her mother on the shearing box where clippers and blades and extension cords are stored. On one sheet of paper, she drew pictures of what she saw. Baby barn swallows in an overhead nest revealed themselves in her hand as a series of open beaks. A wavy line was a rooster's comb, and a collection of round dots signified a sheep sneezing. It all makes perfect sense when Nicki explains it.

On another piece of paper, Nicki draws straight lines. Four in a row and then a diagonal line across. Each line represents a ewe that has been sheared. Each diagonal is a five, two fives are as many fingers as Nicki can count. So each set of two boxes of lines is a bundle. At three, the child has mastered the principles of "the new math."

When the fleeces have been "skirted" (the polite term for removing dung tags), they are folded and stuffed into caterpillar-like burlap sacks. Compacting the wool is an art. One shepherd I know built a twenty-foot tower specifically for stuffing wool bags. Each fleece was drawn to the top of the tower through a series of ropes, pulleys and hooks. Then a designated wool stuffer at the top of the tower loaded the wool into the hanging bag, poking it to the bottom with an extendable window washing handle fixed with a weight instead of a wiper. Inevitably, the handle ended up lodged in the bag with the wool when the wool bag fell to the ground.

Instead, Judy uses Nicki. Dad Steve rolls back the burlap sack to a manageable size and he and I start stuffing. Then Nicki dances and prances on the wool, gyrating it to the bottom of the bag. Judy calls it the "wool war dance."

Each sack can hold twenty fleeces comfortably, but Nicki sees this as a challenge. When it is time to tie off the giant bag and hoist it into the truck, she crawls in sideways and pushes the core of the wool down. At twenty-three fleeces she is usually satisfied.

Nicki has lambs of her own at home, and bunnies and a cat named Rags. Doing chores is as natural to her as breathing. Every day she watches her parents work together. She is never bored.

Judy tells a story about taking her daughter into a coffee shop in the middle of a day of shearing.

"Your child smells like a sheep," the cashier said snootily when they picked up their take-out lunch.

"Thank you," said Nicole, without missing a beat. "I'm a little farm kid, you know."

Barnyards and
Basketball Heads

ONE OF THE THINGS I DISLIKED ABOUT WORKING IN AN
office was the politics — the politics of appearance, the
politics of promotion and the politics of windows, coat
racks and corner offices as definitions of worth. Every day
some back-stabbing plot seemed to be hatching in some
cubicle.

Allegiances, allegations and arbitrations can make the
workplace almost as treacherous as an abattoir. Skirt too
short, off with her head. Voice too squeaky, banished to
the mail room. Getting long in the tooth, bite the early-
retirement bullet. And the boss is seldom a hero. I once
worked in an office where the titular supervisor was dis-
respectfully known as "Old Basketball Head." The pri-
mary function of the staff seemed to be constructing
scenarios that would spell his demise. The cruelty of office
life was something I thought I could avoid on the farm.

But even the barnyard has its politics. Witness the
phenomenon of chickens in a pen. If one decides to lie in a
corner, ten others want to be there as well. So they pile on

top of each other, suffocating the bottom layer. The only way to survive is to claw your way to the top of the heap. Sound familiar?

And chickens do not tolerate weakness any more than office "team players" tolerate slackers. If one bird develops a bad leg, for example, word spreads through the coop with the same speed as derogatory e-mail. The injured bird is on the outs. The others stand apart in groups, clucking privately. Then they take turns as tormenters. At first, they just sneak up from behind and peck the weak one. Then they progress to bullying it in packs. Without supervision, such behaviour leads to murder. In an office, it becomes a pink slip or a transfer.

Pigs raised in confinement are the biggest bullies of all. Once they are weaned, the future wieners are corralled in fattening pens where the only thing they are supposed to do is eat. Like workers assigned to an assembly line, boredom sets in. Soon they are quite literally at each other's throats. You do not find this behaviour in pigs that are left to roam in a pasture where they can root around and explore their own creativity. Diversification of routine creates happy production units — Principles of Management 101.

Horses are the same. My friend Cheryl's extremely sociable equi turned to vandalism when she left them alone during the day to go to work. Even though they had a whole pasture to roam, Sunshine and Morningstar would stand in the barn and apply themselves to the task of pulling boards away from the stall walls. They were afflicted with the same loveless boredom that turns office workers into pencil pilferers and washroom graffiti artists. Cheryl solved the problem by hanging two Frisbees from the barn ceiling. The horses had hours of fun whacking them around with their upraised noses. Show them something new, show them that you care — put a ping pong table in the lunch room.

Cattle and geese may look as though they move in cohesive groups, but spend some time watching and you will observe a hierarchy of authority. It happens quickly and often without warning. Two geese will fly at each other, honking and screaming. Then they will walk off in different directions, with the gaggle following the one who made the best display. An old cow will look up from the salt block and make a beeline for the heifer grazing ahead of her. After broadsiding the innocent youngster into a windless state, old Bossy goes back to licking salt as though nothing had happened. It is called learning your place.

Sheep may be the most corporate of all animals. Innovation intimidates them and they would follow a leader over a cliff to avoid making a false step. Rams only bang heads when there is a threat of a merger or takeover. However, ewes butt each other over serious things such as, "whose blade of grass is this anyway." To the victor go the spoils, and so on.

Yet sometimes I walk through the barnyard and all I see is a well-integrated community of gentle creatures involved in pastoral pursuits that I have established for them. Heads turn, ears perk and they greet me in their languages of contentment. At least I hope that is what is going on. I would hate to think that every "cock-a-doodle-do" actually means, "Here comes Old Basketball Head."

Of Mint and Mayhem

I HAVE NEVER BEGRUDGED THE ODD WEED IN THE garden. A little mayhem adds some humanity to those straight neat rows that start out looking like something from a trigonometry book. If there was nothing to do in the garden except admire the neatness and pick the bounty, I might as well go to the supermarket. And who can ever tell where the wild pumpkin is going to crop up.

My first few gardens were so huge I could spend half a day rototilling between the rows and still have hoeing to do. Then I tried all sorts of weed-free methods, including laying down thick beds of straw between the rows to smother the weeds and mulch naturally. This worked brilliantly until the stray seeds in the straw came to life and I had a sprout festival at hand.

I learned to use a combination of whatever I think will work, including chickens and disincluding chickens at my whim. You see, chickens love weed sproutlets and they love to root out the assorted bugs in the ground. They also create their own nitrogen-rich fertilizer. So if I want to clear a plot of ground for future gardening, I confine the chickens to it as their range. Every week I rototill the chicken range, turning up bugs and worms for the chickens. The weed seeds sprout faithfully, only to be recycled by the chickens. By fall the chickens are fine, fat and well pleased with themselves, and after a final tilling the plot will be virtually weed-free and fertilized for spring planting.

That is the theory. It usually works well until the day before I harvest the tomatoes. Then the chickens break through the mesh that separates them from the real garden and they peck holes in every other ripe tomato. So I plant extra tomato plants on the other side of the house, where the chickens cannot see them.

I am now so accustomed to growing "secret" gardens that I do not even think of them as secret anymore. Ask me why a plot of corn grows behind the flowerbed where poppies, yarrow, lilies and red hot pokers form the backdrop, and all I can say is, "the horses won't think to look there." This is because just as sure as biennials bloom every other year, the horses are bound to find their way into the garden for half an hour when the corn is ripe. If I am not fast enough, the whole crop will be trampled or digested. Then there will be some salvation in having the secret plot. If the horses fail, I will have all the more for the freezer.

I no longer even think about the fact that there is a small plot of red-leaf lettuce in the flowerbed next to the pansies, just in case some groundhog finds the real stuff in the garden. Basil and parsley grow just beside the front steps where even the most bold goose will not nibble it.

And flowering cabbages smile out everywhere, their huge heads bowing like something out of *Little Shop of Horrors*.

Years ago a friend gave me a pot of mint. She warned me to plant it far away from anything I treasured and to confine it strictly to the pot. But it looked so lame, so harmless and so small. I whacked its tiny roots into a flowerbed, expecting nothing but a small whiff of fragrant green to emerge in one quiet spot.

But mint is the wildest and most wiry of all herbs. It has survival instincts that are so profound one suspects that it could survive nuclear holocaust. You can pull it out of the ground by its roots and sift through the soil until you truly believe every fibrous strand is gone for good — two days later there will be a brand new sprout of mint.

I have tried releasing the chickens in the mint. But they do not care much for the peppermint-scented sprouts. The horses will not touch the stuff. Even the sheep deliberately graze around it. So today, I have a mint garden.

It is bounded by rocks and anything else I can think of to confine the pervasive stuff. It just spreads. After years of cursing it, of trying to control it, stop it and kill it, I have decided to simply contemplate the mayhem that is mint.

There is some satisfaction in freely scattering mint leaves around a dessert of baked pears with ice cream. Tarting lamb up with mint sauce has always seemed an abomination to me. If it must be done, all the better to be able to add the authenticity of chopped green leaves to the sweetness. Mint adds zest to tea, and a julep is nothing at all without a large infusion of leafy juices. When the mint garden overtakes all reasonable boundaries of companion living, I mow it down.

Like the wild pumpkin vine that spreads across the middle of a garden row, the mint is a reminder that nature has its own mysterious survival mechanisms. Once triggered, the greater one struggles against it, the larger it looms. Far better to sit back and accept that some roots grow deeper than others.

Catch a Falling Bale

HAYING CAN MAKE YOU CRAZY. AT THE BEST OF TIMES, it is hot, sweaty work. At the worst of times, it is a rush against the rain.

The Moose and I did not know this when we signed up for our first haying. The neighbours said it was a communal activity and everyone helped everyone. So we showed up one promising July morning ready to learn how to bring in the hay.

It was going to be a scorcher of a day. I wore a halter top and shorts. Moose wore his bathing trunks and a big T-shirt with the arms cut off. We could work on our muscles and our suntans at the same time.

Before we set off on the haywagon someone handed us gloves with the fingers cut off at the tips. They fit, sort of. We clapped our hands in delight and posed for the camera shot of our first hay day.

There was some discussion among the men about what sort of bales we would be hauling back. Apparently, there were a number of settings on the baler that ranged from lightweight to heavyweight. The lightweight bales were called "ladies bales." Moose knew that I would have none of that and insisted that we could handle whatever was thrown at us.

"Done by noon," we shouted gaily, as we bounced down the lane on the wagon with a young lad who was going to supervise us.

The field was a good fifteen acres of what looked to be flat land. Cut hat lay in windrows that fluffed in the breeze under three puffs of cloud overhead. In the swamp beside the field, red-winged blackbirds made pitch with their high-sounding calls.

The bales of hay started shooting out of the hay binder with a certain regularity. I marvelled at the notion that some inventor has figured out a way to scoop dehydrated blades of grass out of the dirt and package them neatly with tied string, but no one has figured out how to automatically fold laundry as it comes out of the dryer. Bales kept coming. Soon all thoughts evaporated in a veil of sweat.

We had about twenty bales neatly stacked on top of each other when the teenager waved his arms and shouted for the tractor to stop. A quick course in hay stacking for idiots followed. We learned to place two bales sideways against one laid frontwards followed by two sideways, unless two frontwards were needed to end the row neatly. Overlaps of frontwards and lengthwise bales on the next layer "tied" the pile into some form of solid mass. The proximity of bales counted, otherwise you could find yourself wedged thigh high in bales halfway up the stack.

Somehow, we managed to load the whole wagon. Moose would not complain, but my body ached. The only expanse of skin not covered with dirt or scrapes or sunburn was underneath my gloves. We returned to the barn in serious need of water, sustenance and body armour.

By this time, four clouds had collected overhead. Cows were lying down in the field, apparently a sure sign of rain to come. We were promptly transferred to a new wagon and handed a thermos of lemonade and a bag of baloney sandwiches.

While we gnawed and supped like hungry barn cats, the men fretted about the weather.

"Can you go any faster?" one asked the Moose. We immediately felt like slackers.

"She can't but I can," he responded. Inwardly, I thanked him, too tired to defend my Amazonian honour.

"Well, can you catch a bale?" came the next question.

"Sure, where do I catch it?" said the Moose, drawing himself to his full height with an enormous creak of his knees. I was proud of the big guy. This was his weekend away from the office. His time to revel in rural bliss. He could have been at home sampling the snap of fresh radishes from the garden and watching me arrange bouquets of peonies, but here he was slogging bales. We were farming.

The baler was adjusted. Long-sleeved cotton shirts and green work pants appeared and we strapped them on. The lemonade jug was filled to the brim. We set out on a mission to fast-track some hay.

The tractor took off over the field with a bounce, and the bales started spewing out. The Moose grabbed them in mid-air and chucked them back toward me. He looked like an action hero on Ritalin.

We had half a wagon stacked when I noticed the pickup trucks at the road edge. There were almost a dozen lining the edge of the field.

"Who's having an auction?" I wondered, but you do not have much time to think when bales are flying at you like giant spiked medicine balls. Frontwards, lengthwise, who cared about making a fancy pattern. I tied off at the end of each row and hoped for the best.

When the tractor finally stopped, Moose and I lay on top of the haywagon, wordless, watching dark clouds drifting together. A raindrop hit my ankle and we scurried to the ground to latch onto the back of the wagon for the short ride back to the barn.

There were many trucks gathered in the yard. We rode the wagon straight into the barn, arriving just before the deluge. Pigeons cooed above the steady staccato on the metal roof.

In the doorway of the barn, a gaggle of hayers watched the rain beat down on the stubble in the fields.

"Catch a good bale, son," one older man said. Two others coughed in agreement.

"Never saw that done before," he added, blowing his nose. Then the whole mass of them started chuckling, shoulders moving up and down, backs bending to the knees. They laughed so hard that their baseball caps fell on the wooden-planked floor.

No one before or since has seen such a display of bale catching. Others have tried and failed. Somewhere between Samson and Babe the Blue Ox, the legend of the

Haying Moose was cast. When large round bales became the fashion, rumour had it that the Moose could roll a whole fieldful into the barn in a morning.

But that is just crazy hay talk. It took him almost all day.

A Case of Domestic Shell Shock

PROVING THAT YOU CAN RECYCLE ALMOST ANYTHING, my neighbour Sarah has found a market for infertile goose eggs.

Every year Sarah hatches hundreds of goslings and other waterfowl. What most people would consider a living room is her incubator. Whole walls are lined with hydro-sucking egg warmers. If it contains life in a shell, Sarah can hatch it.

But some eggs do not contain life. All sorts of variables from a change in feed to a change in season can result in an infertile egg. Those that fail to show signs of embryonic life after a certain number of days are rejects. Having been subjected to slow heating, they are no good for eating, but Sarah turns their loss into a profit by selling the big eggs to a woman who hollows them out and paints them for Easter. Sarah makes more selling one barren goose egg than most farmers make selling a dozen fresh chicken eggs.

I wish she could figure out a way to turn my dormant wild turkey eggs into gold.

The problem is that my wild turkeys are an oxymoron — domestic wild turkeys. Hatched in incubators themselves, they are strictly specimens of what used to grow abundantly in the wild. Gradually, the natural wild turkey population is increasing, but my domestically raised wild turkeys would not have a clue about what a balanced diet is if it does not come from a feed mill.

Still, the hen turkeys lay eggs. I have harvested some and hatched a few. As day-olds, the poults show some hint of the wild. Baby cock birds, for example, will lower their tiny wings and shake them along the top of the wood shavings as notice of their territorial rights when the great giant hand fills the feeder in the brooding cage. The wattles of full-grown males turn from purple to red when they feel threatened, and the display they make with their wings sounds like the rattling of tree branches. But if you put a pair of domestic wild turkeys two storeys up in a tree, I venture to say it would take a forklift to rescue them.

Turkey eggs taste almost the same as chicken eggs, a touch darker in the yolk, perhaps. When they are laying, my two hens produce an egg a day. Usually they stop in the late spring, but one year the eldest bird, Hortense, decided she would keep on laying and sit on her eggs.

The broody hen flattened herself over a shallow depression in the earth where she laid her eggs. For weeks I did not see Hortense move. The cock bird flew at me when I filled their feeder, which was highly uncharacteristic for him. One male, Bourbon, has been noted for displays of violence, but his son Hector actively enjoys human company. He once attempted to grab me by the back of the neck and mate with me when I was painting the base of the pen.

Hortense was truly dedicated to her eggs; the problem was that she did not rotate them. The heat eggs need to develop is one thing. Distributing it evenly involves turning the eggs every few hours, no matter how slightly. My incubator has a small motor attached to the egg trays that tilts the egg racks automatically. Hortense just sat there, hugging herself to her eggs with a maternal deliberateness that was not going to hatch a thing.

Six weeks went by. The eggs should have hatched after twenty-eight days or so. Armed with a garbage can lid and sporting a hard hat, I entered the pen. Hector made no protest. Apparently he had grown tired of playing protector. When I took off the hard hat, he tried to mate with it.

Hortense held firm to her eggs. I shoved my hand underneath her and felt roughly a dozen eggs. When I tried to gently remove one, she grabbed my wrist and nearly broke the skin. I got the message.

Hortense sat and sat and sat on those eggs. No amount of cajoling or poking from outside of the pen could convince her to give up the ghost and get on with her life.

Then one day I heard a loud bang from the turkey pen. Then a squawk, another bang and a flutter of wings. Hector was terrified. Hortense was flapping around frantically, jumping up to her perch and then returning to her eggs. When she saw me she plopped on the eggs and tried to pretend nothing had happened. Bang! It happened again. This time I watched her go straight into the air. What we had here was a hot egg explosion.

I wore industrial-strength gloves and two layers of sweatshirts along with my hard hat and coveralls when I retrieved Hortense and put her into another pen with the shell-shocked Hector. The only thing I was missing was a gas mask, and I sorely missed having one. Rotten eggs are one thing, exploding rotten eggs are more like stink-bomb grenades.

Hortense did not lay another egg all summer. I would not blame her if she post-traumatically suppressed eggs for the rest of her life. If she ever decides to lay more than an omelette, I plan to diffuse the whole lot of them and paint them for Easter.

She Swims with the Turtles

WHILE THE FARMERS AROUND ME ARE BUSY HARVESTING and the combines churn in the fields, the vacationers are busy getting on with the task of having a holiday at a furious pace.

Just down the road there are a couple of little lakes and an eighteen-hole golf course surrounded by several thousand summer campers who lodge themselves in all manner of tent or trailer in a sort of stacked-together-outdoor-experience whose common bond is *eau de mosquito* repellant. They stake their place on a few feet of sand and try to commune with nature.

Occasionally, I will slip the bridle on the horse and ride bareback over the hayfield next to the golf course to see how the nature lovers are doing. I get a fairly good view of the seventeenth hole from a hilly mound where groundhogs lie around in the sun. The little carts tootle from hole to hole with foursomes and twosomes in pastel shirts, shorts and visor caps. Old Lady has no idea what to make of it.

I cannot get too close to the campground itself. The sight of a palomino horse causes a sensation. The campers swarm out of their canvas and tin abodes at the sight of anything that could potentially become part of their vacation experience.

Kids always want a ride and everyone has a million questions about what horses eat and how long they live and why do they sleep standing up. Then there is a general scramble to find a carrot to feed the sleeping horse, but in my experience I find that summer campers rarely travel with carrots. Lady often ends up nibbling on a hot dog bun.

I once caused a real kaffufle by taking the horse swimming.

My neighbour, Elwood, shares a pond with the campers. It is a shallow, mud-bottomed affair that supports a small school of fast-swimming, multi-coloured little fish that we call pumpkin seeds because they are oval-shaped and flat as flounders. Mostly, the pond is home to an actively breeding colony of mosquitos and deer flies, which is what drove Lady and I into the water.

Nobody goes swimming in the pond because of the snapping turtles. Legend has it that the entire bottom of the pond is covered with toothsome turtles just looking for a juicy ankle to chomp. There is nothing Elwood likes better than telling a bunch of greenhorns about the time a posse of snapping turtle hunters came all the way from Tennessee to harvest the hard-shelled horrors.

"They were snapper hunters. That's all they did. Took the live turtles back to Tennessee and sold them for gumbo stew — big bucks in turtles. Course its illegal these days," was his usual opening.

"They had steel snares and sabres and long poles with knives stuck to the ends, but they couldn't get old Horace."

Anyone who has heard the story knows that Horace is the turtle equivalent of the Loch Ness monster. The first time I heard the tale, Elwood said Horace was the size of a snow-shovel scoop. In subsequent tellings, he has grown to have the circumference of a tandem-truck tire.

"They'd go out at night on a big old raft with lights to draw the turtles to them," Elwood would explain. "Turtles'd pop their heads up and then they'd lasso them, jump in the water and wrestle them into burlap sacks — turtles clawing them up and down their arms. One of the snappers chewed his way out of the bag and bit a hole right through a steel-toed boot. But it didn't bother those fellas, no sir. Not one of them had a full set of fingers."

As the story goes, the Tennessee turtle hunters had a raft full of bagged snappers on board when Horace reared his fearsome head.

"Those boys never saw the like of it. Old Horace headed for that raft so fast that he raised a wave behind him. They didn't have a snare big enough to fit over his head. Horace rammed into the raft and started ripping chunks out of it."

There ensues a good deal of thrashing, gnawing and tearing. In the end, Horace sinks the raft and liberates his fellow turtles, leaving the turtle hunters to hightail it back to Tennessee with a variety of appendages missing or damaged.

To prove that Horace is still out there, Elwood points out that loons will not land on the pond, and loons are smart birds.

So folks got fairly excited when they saw Lady and me swimming across the pond on a hot and buggy day.

A hoard of mosquitos and deer flies had descended on us when we rode through the woods to the pond. Lady's tail was swatting double time and I was trying to hang on to the reins with one hand and clear a path through the bugs with the other. By the time we got to the water's edge we were both quite loony.

Horses do not generally take it upon themselves to go for a swim, but I had no trouble coaxing Lady into taking the plunge.

Once we got past the mud bottom, it was clear sailing. I kind of floated over her back, clinging to her mane and plucking the deer flies from her tender ears. The water was cool and clear. Lady had no trouble galloping weightlessly through the water as we headed for the far shore.

The whole swim might have lasted ten minutes, but it was enough time for a crowd to gather. People were waving their arms and shouting. Two golf carts left the fairway in mid-hole to follow the commotion.

Dripping, Lady and I emerged from the pond. I slid off her back and she shook her whole body like a wet dog, sending droplets flying all over the pristine pastels of the golfers. My soaking blue jeans suddenly felt like a dead weight. But at least we were surrounded by campers coated in bug repellant. Not a deer fly in sight.

"You sure are lucky Horace didn't get you," said a freckle-faced kid as he stroked Lady's neck. Someone pulled out a bag of marshmallows and the horse glommed them down like Pablum.

I had not even thought about the snapping turtles. I

remembered looking into the water and seeing nothing on the bottom, just an underwater moonscape without so much as a rock or a weed in evidence.

Then Elwood roared up in his pickup truck.

"You are one lucky woman," he announced. "But that horse is even luckier."

I knew something was coming, but with Elwood you just never know where the ball is going to land. He circled Lady slowly, making sucking sounds through his pursed lips and rubbing his cheeks in wonder.

"He almost gotcha, didn't he darlin'," he said clapping his hand on Lady's damp rump and holding her dripping white tail. "Don't worry, a horse's tail grows back in no time and it looks like he just got a grip on a few inches — good thing you kept movin'."

Now I know for a fact that Lady's tail was the same length it has always been, although Elwood's nose seemed to grow with every word. But there is no point in desecrating a legend, especially when you have become a part of it.

Lady and I dried in the sun while we rode home.

My last vision of Elwood was of him perched on a picnic table with a hot dog in one hand and the other pointing to a spot at the far side of the pond.

"Notice there's no beaver dams in the whole pond," I heard him say. "That's cause old Horace is always biting their tails off. Yessir, people think we got a lot of groundhogs around here but all we've got is a bunch of beavers without their tails."

The Soup Ladle Rescue

THE BARN WAS EMPTY. THE SHEEP AND THE HORSES had all taken it upon themselves to spend the late days of summer in the shade of the back pasture, where they forage for fallen apples from the wild apple trees. So I was surprised to hear a small racket of peeping coming from the far corner of the barn. The baby barn swallows had long ago swooped from their nest in the rafters. I wondered what could be left.

That particular area of the barn is rather dark. In the spring, it is the favoured spot for ewes to lie down and deliver their lambs. But in the summer, it becomes what a neighbour's little girl calls, "the place where spiders live." In the few rays of sunlight that filtered through to the corner, I could see the big, filigree webs the spiders had been spinning. With some regret and some timidity, I chopped my way through their handiwork with my broom, looking for the source of the peeping.

The peeping was loudest in the corner, where a covering of plywood separates the exterior metal barn walls from damage when the tractor clears out the manure. At the bottom of the four-foot high plywood — in a gap about the diameter of a garden rake — I could see the soft beige feathers of a tiny Old English Game hen, puffing her wings over a fresh hatch of thumb-sized chicks.

As I walked back to the house to get a flashlight for a better look, I pondered the dilemma. The secretive hen had selected a truly secretive place to brood her eggs. Unfortunately, she had also selected a space that offered no exit until her chicks could fly. No exit also meant no food and no water.

Moose, joined me to analyze the problem. The whole idea of a new batch of chicks so late in the season had him all excited.

In the glare of the flashlight, the hen moved. We counted eight tiny heads. But the narrowness of the gap and the height of the dividing wood was such that even the long arm of the Moose could not reach them. We contemplated ways and means of lowering food and water. We thought about cutting a hole in the wood so the birds could make their escape.

Nothing seemed practical, until I thought of the soup ladle.

Moose could not ease more than his arm down the wooden wall. However, I figured if I stood on a tall metal pail I might be able to lean further down the gap with my short arms and use the ladle to scoop the chicks out.

So, while he trained the flashlight, I balanced on the pail and hoisted my right shoulder into the breach where I slashed through a cloud of cobwebs with my soup ladle.

I was standing on my tiptoes and the ladle was just

inches away from scooping up a chick when my right breast shifted down into the gap, giving me just the depth I needed. A brownish ball of fluff fairly rolled right into the ladle and I tried to draw it slowly up.

Quickly I discovered that any movement I might make would have to be sideways, since the shift of my bosom had lodged me firmly in the gap. So while I teetered on the old bucket, I ladled the chicks sideways into the Moose's waiting hand.

The hen found all of this most distressing, and made several assaults on the ladle with her beak and her tiny wings. When the nest was empty, I finally managed to clutch her back and pass her up to be reunited with her babies.

Extricating me from the gap was another matter. I wiggled and teetered on the bucket to no avail. Finally, Moose suggested greasing me with salad oil, which started us both laughing. Then something shifted, freeing my boob, soup ladle and all.

We put the chicks and the hen into the pail and took them to a pen. Game birds are smaller and even more delicate than the Banties that strut around farmyards like miniature chickens. The babies were so tiny that even the smallest of chick waterers that I had on hand would have been so deep that one false step could lead to a drowning.

Moose solved the problem with shallow pop bottle caps, weighted with pennies glued to the bottom so they could not tip over.

In no time, the hen was wandering around scratching in the dirt and pecking in the feed dish — teaching and eating at the same time. When the chicks rest, they flock under her wings. Sometimes all you can see of the eight of them is one little head with blazing dark eyes or one little chick foot straggling beyond its mother's fine feathers.

People occasionally ask me where I go for a summer vacation. Well, I do not go much of anywhere. Maybe, like the sheep and the horses I will wander to the back pasture to find apples, but otherwise, it is best to stick close to the farm.

After all, a hen with a new brood in a no-exit zone cannot call 911. And a farmer never knows when it might be time to get out the soup ladle and perform a rescue mission.

The Summer of Love

*I*T IS HARD TO LEAVE THE FARM FOR LONG PERIODS OF time. I have been lucky enough to have neighbours who are willing to pitch-hit on overnight trips, even weekends, when business, family obligations or windfall World Series tickets demand a sojourn. Still, it takes days of preparation. You try to think of anything that could go wrong and cut it off at the pass — replacing that barn light bulb that must be on the edge of virtual burnout, for example. If an animal is sick or due to deliver, you just do not go.

Even in the summer when the sheep and horses are in the pasture feeding themselves and drinking from an automatic waterer, there is always the chance that a lamb will stray or a gosling will fall into a groundhog hole. Such worries have caused me to have guilt attacks in the middle of a Rolling Stones concert and have prompted the urge to phone home as soon as a bride and groom have said "I do."

I can take a writerly meeting in the city, but the fol-low-through is something I can do from the farm. So when the career opportunity of a lifetime presented itself, I was in a quandary because it meant I would have to spend five days a week for half of a summer working in the city.

Farm economics being what they are, I did not have much of an option. So, I started looking for a full-time relief shepherd. I might as well have been looking for ears on a snake.

Coincidentally, one of my closest high school friends called. Angie has always been a manic whirlwind. She is the kind of woman who will do back flips down a bar on a bet. I have seen this, personally. She writes poetry and music, which she recites, sings and plays with the passion of her Russian ancestry. A quick study, she once married a chess player and in no time she herself was representing Canada at chess Olympiads. The marriage ended in checkmate, but her board game skills led to a job in Europe managing the World Chess Federation. She has sold everything from pianos in Brussels to BMWs in Hong Kong.

I have learned that her phone calls can be anything from a 2 a.m. "Psst Marsha, I'm calling from Rick's Cafe. I'm with Bobby Fisher and he's wearing a fake beard" to "They want me to go to Beijing. I can't go to Beijing. There's no night life, just one darn Planet Hollywood." But this time her phone call was about coming home and being in love.

From my standpoint it was perfect. She and her first high school flame, Derek, had reacquainted. While they were sorting out where and how they would plan a life together, they would be delighted to spend the summer taking care of the farm. On weekends, I could come home to all things bright and beautiful, and they could roam the countryside in search of their own heaven on earth. I breathed a sigh of relief. One hitch: they had no experience whatsoever.

Angie, Derek and a monstrously huge cat named Charlie arrived a week early to acclimate themselves. They brought Wellington boots, an electric piano and a wok that came all the way from Macao. Angie wanted to start farming immediately. She rushed to the paddock where the horses were grazing and leaned over the fence calling, "Here horsie, here horsie." I did not have a nanosecond to warn her about the strand of electric fencing at the top of the fence. That was her first shock of farm life.

Angie and Derek spent the next few days following me around and making lists. They listed the number of scoops of grain I gave the horses and the bin that it came from. They listed the number of brown eggs that we collected. They noted the identifying marks and location of animate and inanimate objects. The red-golden pheasant was "male: red and gold with some blue and green feathers; female: brown, no long tail. 2nd bird run. Name: Mao and Mrs. Mao, from Manchuria!" A chicken feeder was, "metal, hanging in back coop. Fill from blue container, wash weekly, use side hose."

And they asked questions. Does the ram bite? Do bees sting chickens? When I told them to toss some grain to the duck every day they asked how many handfuls. Angie started reading sheep health books and querying me about things like the difference between foot rot and foot and mouth disease.

At night, Derek drew maps and Angie made schedules. They charted every inch of the farm, noting each and every strand of electric fencing. A blueprint of the garden recorded the rows by number and tabled the dates when the peas and carrots should be ready. Chores were equally divided. Derek to brush the horses on Mondays, Angie on Tuesdays. Mow the lawn — Derek; weed the garden — Angie, and so on.

All of this attention to detail made me start to realize how complex the whole operation actually was. I made up my own list of contacts and phone numbers in case of any emergency from dishwasher meltdown to rabies.

My first week of city work passed uneventfully. I called home morning, noon and night. All was well. Diva Dog chased Charlie Cat up a tree, but everything else was tickety-boo. When I arrived home that first weekend, vegetables from the garden were steaming in the wok and Derek was grilling lamb chops to perfection. The sheep grazed happily in their field and the horses shone golden in the sunset. Diva sat obediently when Angie told her to, even though Charlie and the barn cats careened right in front of her after a chipmunk.

The lovebirds loved farming. It suited the bloom of their mood. The next day they showed me their routine. Hand in hand they strode to the barn, calling each passing chicken by name. Groucho the duck quacked happily in their direction. He never did that to me. One little lamb — a darling thing with a button of a nose — came over to the fence to give Angie a nuzzle.

"There now Chelsea," said Angie, bending to give the lamb a hug. "I hope you don't mind, I just call her Chelsea because she's sweet, like the buns, you know." I knew.

Assured that they had done a terrific job, off they flew

to spend the day antique hunting. I plopped myself on a lawn chair and wondered which big heavy book I should start reading now that I worked in the city and had time on my hands.

And so it went for weeks on end. I reduced my telephone calls home to one a day. On weekends, I puttered around in the garden and watched the lawn grow. There was plenty of time left over to go horseback riding. Angie made enough strawberry jam to last for two winters and Derek rebuilt the barn door that had been sticking for years. When it rained, they went outside together and danced through the flowerbeds, singing and laughing like Dead Heads at a sixties love-in. They had terrific suntans.

By the time my job assignment ended, Angie and Derek had found their dream homestead. When they drove down the laneway with Charlie sitting in the back window, the egg-fed barn cats came close to tears. I turned to find perfection in whatever I beheld and wondered how I could possibly manage to keep it that way.

The next day potato beetles invaded the garden. Two nights later, raccoons levelled half a row of corn. A heat wave followed and the chickens were of no mind to lay. One ewe started limping. Diagnosis: foot rot. I treated the whole flock by walking them through a formalin foot bath. Those who did not want to walk through, I pushed through. Consequently I was also foot-rot free, and knee-rot free and elbow-rot free. Then it rained for three solid days and the lawn grew a foot.

The summer of love had ended. Chelsea had doubled in size. Groucho duck went back to being grouchy. It was back to life as usual and I was not about to leave it soon.

Fall

Folly Comes to Fruition

I HAVE EATEN AN APPLE. TO MOST IT WOULD HAVE seemed a rather ordinary fruit; red, round. No big deal. But I have been waiting a long time for this particular apple.

It is not as though there are no apples on the farm. I can view the aged survivors of a pioneer orchard from the kitchen sink window — gnarled boughs glazed with ice in winter, pink-white blossoms in spring, green fruit trinkets, through the leaves of summer and rosy, swelling apples in the fall.

And there are wild apple trees all over the place, on fencelines and in the middle of pasture fields. They have a certain mystery. I wonder what seed they came from and how long they have lived here? Nothing about wild apples is predictable. They come in all sorts of flavours from sugary smooth to mouth-puckering tart.

I have always liked apples, but seldom craved them because they seem to be so predominant in my life. From a couple of trees, I can gather hundreds of apples of all sizes. Over the years I have had larders filled with apple derivatives — apple jelly, apple chutney, apple butter and, of course, applesauce.

Still, gathering apples is a lot of work. And wild apples tend to be a bit rough. They can be pockmarked, nibbled by bugs or worm-eaten. The biggest, brightest fruits always seem to be at the top of the tree, one ladder step out of reach.

Every year the apples seem higher and the ladder seems shorter. And something is getting rickety — it could be the ladder, but maybe it is me.

So I decided to create an orchard of dwarf apple trees that would flourish right next to the garden at the front of the house. I have watched all sorts of people as they age and there seems to be a certain amount of shrinkage that goes on over the years. At least with dwarf trees, I figured I might still be tall enough to pick apples when the pension cheques start.

The orchard was planted eight years ago. Five trees is all that it is. The whole deal cost me about $150, and I do not expect my apple harvest will ever pay me a dime. The trees have taught me about pruning and fertilizing. I have stripped and burned the dreaded tent caterpillars from their slender boughs. I have wrapped their trunks to protect them from the ravages of winter bunnies and frost. In times of fungal peril, I have mixed organic pesticides with water and washed the leaves of each threatened tree.

Eight years of this, and finally, one tree on the north side of the orchard produced an apple.

It was a McIntosh.

I looked at it for a long time, hanging there from a

delicate stem, defying gravity. When I finally reached up to pluck it, I had visions of Eve in the Garden but I knew that my apple was imbued only with good intentions. I nudged it gently and the apple plopped into my hand.

After holding it for an appropriate time and marvelling at the perfect imperfection of its beauty — one side larger than the other and the red skin somewhat streaked with gold — I cored it and cut it into bite-sized strips.

The Moose has always considered my little orchard something of a folly — a non-event — a bit like growing sunflowers only to have all the seeds devoured by blue jays before we even get a few to add to the granola mix. But when folly comes to fruition, the reward is sweet. I shared the bounty of my harvest with him, and we both pronounced it the best apple ever eaten. Next year I may have enough to make an apple pie.

Almost certainly, by the time my pension cheques start arriving, the dwarf orchard should be producing bushels of apples. It is hard to envision that happening right now, but there is some comfort in knowing that as I shrink into my Golden Years, I will always have apples within easy reach.

The World's Largest All-Female Marching Kazoo Band

IT STARTED IN THE MOUNT ROYAL TAVERN, WHERE many things are started and few are realized. Tim "Spider" Noonan and the boys were halfway in the trough on a warmish sort of evening, when an attractive young woman known as Spike dropped by with a few girlfriends. Boys being boys, they got a bit giddy thinking of ways to engage Spike and her entourage in conversation. Spider drummed his fingers so hard that every glass of beer on the table became effervescent. Then he came up with the idea.

"Can you ladies hum?" he inquired, raising his eyebrows expectantly.

"Anyone can hum," said Spike.

"Good. You can try out for the marching band," came his rejoinder.

The women laughed, as he knew they would. Thus engaged, someone asked, "Who ever heard of a marching band that hums?"

"The band doesn't hum, exactly," said Spider. "They

hum into kazoos and march. Haven't you ever heard of the World's Largest All-Female Marching Kazoo Band?"

There is nothing quite like the thrill of a marching band. But once you reach a certain age, the dream of ever being part of one dissipates, especially if you play the piano. The kazoo was a back door to a dream and the Homecoming Parade for the Old Boys and Girls Reunion was fast approaching.

The first gathering of aspiring marching women kazooists took place at Minto Meadows, the activities headquarters of the U.I.C. Flyers Social Club, of which Spider Noonan is convenor. About fifty women showed up. Some came with their mothers, some had children in tow and some just brought a cooler. Local retailers noted a run on kazoos the likes of which they had never seen. By the end of that first day, everyone knew their instrument. As Bacall said to Bogart: "You just put your lips together and blow."

The kazoo marching band evolved into a model of democratic procedure mingled with chaos. Two drummers, a cow bell player and a triangle tinkler volunteered to set the pace. Spider got to play the cymbals because it was his idea. Women who had been passing each other in supermarkets for years without speaking marched side by side, touching fingertips to maintain proper distances and debating the arch-support merit of various types of running shoes. At least a dozen women could do a passing impression of Phil Silvers as Sergeant Bilko. "To the leeheft, right, leeheft. Leeheft...Leeheft."

Selecting marching music was another matter. Someone suggested the Disney theme "It's a Small World" and kazoos were heard to gag. The Irish contingent lobbied for "MacNamara's Band," and won. Polka enthusiasts fought for "Roll Out the Barrel." Everyone agreed it gave them happy feet. "Three Blind Mice" as a rondo worked at a standstill but floundered when married to marching, as did The Beatles' "Oo Blah Dee." Everyone agreed that "When the Saints Go Marching In" was a natural. Three songs would do it. The whole parade was only about six blocks long.

Word spread and soon the ranks of the kazoo band swelled to one hundred strong. Friends brought friends into the band and co-workers brought co-workers. Spider's two daughters joined the band, as did his ex-wife and his ex-girlfriend. The ex-wife brought her three sisters, and one of them ended up leading the band. If there was nepotism, it took a circuitous route.

Leading the band was a bit like organizing a day-care centre for a bus trip.

"Everyone hold your kazoo in your left hand," Band Leader Vi would begin, waving her baton. "No not that left hand, your other left hand."

Vi's baton looked suspiciously like a broom handle with a gold papier mâché knob on the end, which was exactly what it was. Sometimes Spider had to crash cymbals to bring order.

"Watch the butt in front of you and keep your distance," Vi commanded as one hundred kazoo-blowing women marched five abreast down the curved laneway of Minto Meadows. When they reached the turn at O'Dwyer's Sideroad, one hundred heads, some permed and some in ponytails, turned to check for traffic — to the left, right, left. And the kazoo band went marching along.

The neighbours came out to watch, and the thrill of having a crowd enthused the marchers. Kids and dogs were a distraction. One entire line of marchers fell out of step and the band had to mark time until they regrouped. The smokers in the bunch heaved and wheezed. Even six blocks was going to be a challenge, but if men in skirts blowing sheep bladders could make it...

"Remember to breathe before you blow," advised one nursing kazooist. "Don't just assume it's a hot flash if you feel red in the face and woozy."

The subject of uniforms arose. To put it delicately, the general consensus was that the supplier would have to understand the meaning of "Extra Large." There was not going to be any spandex marching in this band. The name of the band was printed in hot pink on white T-shirts featuring a kazoo with musical notes over top of it. Co-ordinate this with white pants, white running shoes and a hot pink visor and you had one sharp dressed marching kazoo band.

At the hot dog roast following the final rehearsal, children ran around playing their mothers' kazoos under shady maple trees. There was discussion about where the band would be positioned in the parade. No one wanted to march behind the riding horses, and especially not behind the draught horses.

Some distance had to be drawn between the kazoo band and the calliope or both musical art forms would be compromised.

It would be a health concern to march in the wake of the exhaust fumes trailing behind the huge transport truck that always gets into the parade just because it is too big for anybody to say "no" to.

"And remember," advised Vi, "the most important thing is to go to the bathroom before the parade starts."

Homecoming celebrations kicked off three days before the parade with a Gigantic Bingo. The next day out-of-town campers began setting up their tents on the front field of the Stinson Farm. Friday was Old Boys and Girls Registration Day, sidewalk sale day and dedication of the Town Bell day. Swimming at the public pool was free and there were almost as many pies at the Presbyterian church salad supper as there were salads. Before the Welcome Home Dance started, the Beard Growing Contest was judged followed by the offer of free shaves for all competitors courtesy of Floyd's Barber Shop.

Only a few kazooists showed up for the pre-parade breakfast at the Legion. Most were too busy pulling out hair curlers and putting in a few final minutes of practice. A sea of pink visors collected in the roadway where the parade was forming. There were a few nervous Nellies in the pack, but they soon got down to focusing on "Leeheft, Right, Leeheft." The Porta-Podies across from the ambulance garage did a brisk business.

Band Leader Vi sported a plume that looked a lot like a feather duster in the back of her visor. Before the parade took off Spider crashed his cymbals.

"Remember it's your right hand that you raise when you say 'hey' at the end of each song," shouted Vi. "If we don't all do it together people will think we're drunk."

Someone reminded her that it was eleven o'clock in the morning and the Bavarian Beer Garden at the curling rink did not even open until two in the afternoon. Someone else suggested marching straight to the curling club. Then the convertible carrying the Dairy Princess started moving and the Largest All-Female Marching Kazoo Band in the land went into parade mode.

To say that it was glorious would be an understatement. They marched with pride, strutting all of their stuff and breathing deeply through their smiles. When the parade came to a brief halt while a Shriner replaced the wheel on his go-kart, the marching band marked time and sang a few choruses of "When the Saints Go Marching In" to the delight of the crowd. Adolescent sons cringed at the sight of their mothers making such a display of themselves. Grandchildren cheered their grannies on. The Old Boys and Girls saw so many familiar faces that their hands grew limp from waving.

At the fairgrounds where the parade ended, the band played "Oo Blah Dee" and a jived-up version of "Three Blind Mice." Husbands congratulated wives, boyfriends were kissed and kids carried on shoulders.

"I love a parade," shouted Spider, and the kazoo band looked up in unison.

"If you can hum a few bars, we can play it," said Spike.

The Barest Hole of All

GROUNDHOG HOLES, RABBIT HOLES AND SNAKE HOLES — there are all sorts of holes in the country and all sorts of critters who live in them. Then there was the day we found the hole of all holes.

My neighbour Elmer found it out in the corner of a hillside where he was digging out sandy soil to even the landscape. Elmer is a fairly laid back fellow. He handles big machinery with easy grace, but when you see him sitting under his apple tree, leaning back with his legs crossed, you would swear he was more akin to a leprechaun than a heavy machinery operator.

Elmer came booting up to the house to announce the discovery of the hole. It was a bigger hole than he had ever seen in these parts and he has been in these parts all of his life. He had never seen the like of it. It was a hole so big it was almost a cave.

Essentially, he wanted a flashlight and some back-up. One never knows what could be in a hole that size. Moose unlocked the shotgun. Although there was no direct talk about it, we were all thinking the same thing. This could be the home of the legendary bear of Minto Township.

I heard about the bear during my first lonely winter on the farm. I was not used to the depth of the silence in the country. Some days the only sounds I heard were the creaking of tree branches and the cries of the blue jays. At night, the great stillness was rarely broken by anything more than the distant hum of a snowmobile, but sometimes I would hear sounds coming from the forest; rumblings that would set the dog barking.

Everyone seemed to have a different version of the bear story but no one had seen it firsthand. The colour of the bear ranged from black to reddish brown. Its size was anything from adult grizzly to cuddly cub. Some folks said it had escaped from a zoo, but there were no zoos for miles around. By my reckoning of the stories I had been told, the bear was now approaching middle age.

We got to the hillside and found the fine deep hole tunnelled into the hill. At first we did not venture close. No sound came from the hole and even the dog was not terribly interested. Every once in a while some loose dirt skittered down the hill and we all leapt back, fearful of an avalanche or some sort of curse that would befall any who entered, just like in the Egyptian tombs.

"Well, we best see if that tunnel from the hole goes anywhere," said Elmer, and we bowed to his authority.

I ran back to the house to get some newspapers. The idea was that we could shove them in the hole and burn them to see if smoke came up anywhere else. We all knew such things could happen, because a hole that deep in the ground had to have an air feed from somewhere. I was selected to install the newspaper because I was the small-est and possibly the quickest — if something should hap-pen. Armed only with a childproof lighter, I entered the hole and did the deed.

We all ran over to the other side of the hill to look for puffs of smoke, but there were none. Elmer examined a few groundhog holes and tried to calculate which one could be the exit point of the main hole, based on the trajec-tory of the arc from the hole to the hillside and such things.

We became more bold and brought a few shovels down to the hole and started digging. The hole was about an oil barrel in diameter, nothing but gravel at the bottom and sandy soil above. Finally, Elmer decided to dig the thing out with his bulldozer to find out where it went.

The machine roared to life and leftover starlings blew out of the trees. He ploughed the bulldozer into the hill and lifted the hole out. It crumbled and the whole hill shook and groaned. I held the dog back, just in case the old bear came out with the hole.

No bear. No bones. Not so much as a sleeping raccoon lived in the hole. We walked away slightly disappointed. Now we had a story to tell at the pub, but no bear to go with it.

A few weeks later, I heard that the bear had been spot-ted in a neighbouring township. Someone else thought they saw the bear at the dump. Children walking home from school claimed the bear walked right past them and went into a ravine. Goose hunting season was about to open and there was concern about the safety of the hunters in a bear-infested landscape. Some folks talked about some animal rights activists coming to town for a rally to urge the humane capture of the bear. No one seemed to recall that bears begin their hibernation in the autumn.

Halloween came and went. Still no sign of the bear. After the destruction of the hole, Elmer left the site alone. In the spring, we will have another look. Holes like that one do not happen for no reason at all. And in the country, there can be bears that live forever, in the barest of holes.

Haute Headgear

WHEN I LIVED IN THE CITY, I HARDLY EVER WORE HATS of any kind. Something furry in winter and something breezy in summer were about it. But on the farm, to every season there is a hat.

Variations on the baseball cap are universally accepted, whether or not baseball is in season. Long into October, the baseball cap is worn. In winter, a version of the baseball cap comes with earflaps. In spring and summer, baseball caps are aerated. A baseball cap can be worn with the brim front-wards, backwards or sideways. In terms of cap etiquette, the sideways wearing of the brim indicates that the bearer is on "half-lock," while a complete reversal of the brim is a "full-lock" situation. These variations generally display them-selves in social circumstances involving libations.

Some hats are "for good" and others are working hats. Straw hats with broad brims are for gardening, while straw fedoras are often suited to haying. If you take the advice of oldtimers, a burdock leaf placed in the dome of a straw hat will help to wick away the steam that rises to the top. However, straw hats generally have a limited lifespan, particularly when they are worn in the company of goats. Cowboy hats are ideal for attending cattle auctions, but unless they are tied down like the Lone Ranger's they often hang up in trees during trail rides.

Winter hats are purely practical. It is written somewhere that 90 per cent of your body heat can escape through the top of your head. Toques are essential and the nice thing about them is that you can layer them under or over other hats. Hats with Velcro fixtures for holding up brims and letting down earflaps offer a whole world of adjustable warmth. Gore-Tex hats and Thinsulate hats start getting pretty fancy for wearing in the barn, but in the howling dead of winter such extravagance can be forgiven. The only winter headgear that can be disconcerting is the full face mask. I wore one in the barn once and the sheep thought I was a stranger.

Still, of all my millinery treasures, it is the shower cap that has proved to be the most universally indispensable. You can be all done up to head for a dance or a visit with friends and decide to take one last trip to the barn to check on things without fear of getting barn-scented hair if you wear a shower cap. Any plain old plastic shower cap will do, as long as the elastic stays firmly in place. And because a shower cap is looser than a bathing cap, your hair stays approximately the way you have styled it. You can even wear curlers under a shower cap.

Unlike fabric hats and caps, a shower cap can be rinsed in soapy water after each use and towel dried, completely odour-free. This makes it particularly attractive during lambing season when rounds of the barn are made

every few hours. There is no point in sullying fresh pil-
lowcases with barn hair when a shower cap offers a cheap
and easy prophylactic solution.

On a farm, headgear is a way of life rather than a
fashion statement. At least that is what I tell myself when
I find myself reaching for the faithful shower cap beside
the alarm clock at 2 a.m. Something furry or something
breezy may have a time and place, but something plastic
can come in awfully handy.

A Tale of Two Tickets

COUNTRY ROADS HAVE A NATURAL SLOWNESS TO THEM that comes with bumps and ruts and loose gravel. There are no lines drawn neatly down the middle. Unless a passing horse and buggy has left some equine marker, country roads tend to be bare of anything except the cloud of dust that flies in the wake of everyone who passes.

You get to know the shape of roads that you travel most frequently. Two deep tracks in the ditch near the end of my lane mark the spot where the carpenter's truck ended up one icy day. That was more than five years ago, but I can still recall how blue the February air turned when the carpenter found out that he had skidded into a swamp.

Along the edge of a hayfield further down the road there is a stump of a maple tree that is a constant reminder of the night there was a stag party at the pig farm. One of the celebrants backed his truck clear across the road and into the tree before leaving. That collapsed old maple kept the wood stove burning for half a winter.

I drive slowly on country roads because that is part of the joy of them.

The plain fact is that I did not even learn how to drive a car until I moved to the country. In the city, I took taxis or found obliging men with cars to take me places. It worked quite nicely. Besides, why would anyone want to drive in the city when all the people who do drive do nothing but complain about traffic and the absence of parking spots?

But the country is different. There is no such thing as a convenience store on the corner. After one week without wheels I was close to having a tizzy. Mennonite children on bicycles had more mobility than I did. So the Moose and I decided to forgo putting a Jacuzzi in the master bathroom. Instead, we bought a turquoise pickup truck for me to use.

It was what you would call an aged pickup truck. At least it was a Ford, which the neighbours thought showed a modicum of taste. I waxed her the first day we got her and the turquoise paint fairly shone.

The truck was a standard, which did not mean much to me at the time. Soon I was shifting gears as though I was born to hand foot co-ordination. I passed my driving test in the old truck and we were bonded. Slow and steady was our credo. I do not think we went further than twenty kilometres in any direction, but that was all we needed.

So about three years later, I was ashamed when I was stopped for speeding on a sideroad that did have a nice neat line painted on it. I was also surprised.

It happened on one of those late autumn days when nothing seems right and every radio station you switch to has a weather announcer who forecasts snow in the cheeriest of voices. Worse, I had decided to do the laundry. Two full hampers of barn clothes, long johns and stiff woollen socks joined me on the front seat of the ancient turquoise pickup. She was still running like a top, but her body was fading fast. I was dressed about the same way the old truck looked, wearing the only clean clothes I had left in the house and hoping the patches would hold.

I could not put the hampers on the floor because certain areas had rusted clear through and the plywood that covered the holes was always shifting. I tried it once and lost two perfectly good socks through the floor.

When the police cruiser passed me coming the other way, I thought the officer who waved at me was just some guy I fox-trotted with at the Kinsmen's beef barbecue in the summer. In fact, he was. I gave him my usual two-fingered salute from the steering wheel. The disconcerting part was that a minute or so later, he was following me with his lights flashing and his hand still waving.

I geared the old truck down and pulled over, checking to see if the laundry was still intact, imagining that I might be trailing some sheet out the window, or worse under the floor board.

Once we got over the formalities of remembrance of barbecues past, the young officer — whom I remembered as exceptionally light on his feet — advised me that I had been going a full twelve kilometres over the speed limit.

Well, I was astounded.

"I didn't think she could go that fast," I told him, in all honesty.

"Well, you seem to be in an awful hurry and you

know this truck can't take that kind of driving," he said, scanning the plywood flooring.

I knew I was supposed to say something about the urgency of my mission and my laundry-distracted feminine state, but I was so darn proud that the old truck had managed such velocity that I forgot my lines. Besides, the smell of stale socks was filling the truck cab sufficiently to impress the officer with the notion of urgency.

"Okay, we'll let you go this time, but slow down and let this be a warning," he said.

The idea of getting a speeding ticket had not caught up to me yet and all of a sudden I realized I was being let off the hook. I was so excited that I knocked over the laundry detergent when I put my ownership papers back into the glove compartment.

I left the scene of my crime in a cloud of dust mixed with laundry detergent that was sifting through the floor boards.

The turquoise truck held on for a couple more years, until she finally fell prey to the rust that never sleeps. I do not know what the final mortal wound was but I do know that she "popped a rad," needed a "valve job" and was "misfiring on three pistons." I suspect any one of those things could bury even the most stalwart pickup half her age.

My next truck was the spiffiest thing you have ever seen. I thought that no truck could ever replace the turquoise Ford in my heart, but this new little filly was a heart-breaker. She was navy and cream, the same colours as the flags at the ploughing match that year. In fact, she was an official ploughing match truck before I got her — complete with ploughing match emblems beside her taillights. No holes in her floor, in fact, her half-ton bed was lined with rubber and she had a tarpaulin top to keep out the rain.

I did not even need to wax the new truck before I took her for that first spin into town. It was a fine fall day. I wore sunglasses and lip gloss and a perfectly matched ensemble.

The unmarked cruiser passed me at the bottom of the hill and there was no waving. By the time I got to the top of the hill, there were flashing lights behind me. An officer who I knew I had never danced with came up to my open window and his portly belly nudged the shiny door of the truck cab.

"Clocked you going ninety-two in an eighty zone, Miss," he said, and I felt ashamed. Surely this new heap could go faster than that on a downhill grade even with me at the clutch.

I retrieved my documents from the pristine dash compartment and watched the officer dutifully note that the ownership had been transferred within the past forty-eight hours.

"Nice truck," he offered and I imagined him on the car lot kicking new truck tires. I was glad my truck would never have to surrender to that sort of abuse ever again.

Briefly, I considered saying something in my defence. But he was watching me, waiting for my learned feminine lines. I could not do it, to myself or to the new truck.

"Just going into town, sir," I said.

From behind his badge, he was sizing me up. Even though my driver's licence showed I was living in the country, it was obvious from my get-up and my gloss that

I had come from outside and thought I was pretty hot stuff, new truck and all. He reached into his pocket and I knew that the law had me in its sights. While he wrote the ticket, I swear I watched a dozen old pickup trucks zoom past us at speeds far exceeding my downhill effort.

The fine was roughly equivalent to the profit I might expect from the sale of one lamb. I accepted it as a sacrifice of some sort to the memory of the old turquoise truck who never got me a ticket.

After that, the new truck and I were bonded in our infamy. At the top of every hill, I would rein her back and check the speedometer, recalling the time that we both seemed fast and far too glorious to be "country." Over the years, we collected a lot of dust together on the sideroads, but we never got another ticket. Country roads bring you down to speed — at the best of times...and the worst.

The Cement Truck Cometh

COULD SOMEONE PLEASE EXPLAIN TO ME THE RELATIONSHIP that men seem to have with cement? The combination of grit, stone and water in the giant tumbler on wheels that we know as a cement truck seems able to capture some primeval masculine heartstring and pluck it directly.

I discovered this phenomenon when we were attempting to construct a pad of cement about the size of a bathtub on which to set a brand new, weather-proof, never-freezing, jim dandy, yellow automatic waterer for the sheep. Expert help was called upon to construct the frame which would contain the cement. It took Mr. McCutcheon and his helper half a day to build a frame worthy of containing the volume of cement required.

You can always rent cement mixers and do it yourself, but that route has its own follies. Inexperience can lead to cracks and other horrors too awful to contemplate.

The key word became "pour," and the source of "the pour" was a cement truck. So I called the sand and cement company that operates within half a mile of my farm and described my needs.

Well, it seems you do not just buy as much cement as you need, instead you must buy a "yard" of the stuff. No one ever adequately explained to me the dimensions of a yard of cement, but they were able to tell me that I would have about half a yard too much.

When a woman starts fooling around ordering cement pours, word gets around. My neighbour Ken "the Hooter" Houston soon caught wind of the plan since he pals with Paul O'Dwyer who drives truck for the cement plant that borders his beef farm.

"Hear you're planning a pour," Hooter said emerging from his truck with his shovel in his hand, even though the cement was not scheduled to arrive for two days.

After inspecting the frame that would enclose the pour and dutifully adding a few shovelfuls of dirt to shore the whole thing up, Hooter turned his attention to the question of what to do with the leftover cement.

Where I would put cement if I had it is not a question that I had ever considered. Perhaps a nice walkway in front of the pheasant pens, maybe a really big bird bath.

Ultimately, Hooter decided we should build a ramp into the barn, smoothing the way for the tractor which had been bumping and jumping every time it went in and out during the barn cleaning days. Hooter brought over some gravel, since apparently cement does not cling well to plain old dirt. Then we took a few pieces of lumber and framed the ramp.

The day of the pour dawned brightly. Hooter came early to announce that Paul O'Dwyer himself would be driving the cement truck, so I had nothing to worry about. Mr. McCutcheon just happened to drop over to check on the frame and my neighbourly town road maintenance supervisor came by to make sure the pour went as planned. As more and more neighbours arrived, I began to wonder if I should be selling tickets.

A cement truck is an impressive sight at close range. The fact that the huge drum rolls slowly at all times gives the whole vehicle an appearance of life. Red-haired O'Dwyer waved to the assembled crew from his perch in the truck cab as he rolled toward the waiting frame.

The first pour took about ten minutes. The cement wriggled and rattled down a sluice that came out of the cement truck like some kind of grey elephant's trunk. Once the frame was filled the men gathered to tap it lightly and smooth the top with trowels. They looked a little bit like pre-schoolers playing with Play-Dough.

The creative work came when all hands gathered at the barn door ramp. Discussion ensued about whether or not the frame Hooter and I had constructed was up to the test, but we decided to pour anyway. The cement truck drum hummed away and the cement oozed out in irregular clumps which were quickly raked and shovelled into an even shape.

"She's a darn fine pour," Hooter proclaimed loudly, turning the rake over to the road maintenance supervisor who was anxiously awaiting his turn. Mr. McCutcheon muttered something about amateurs and ran back to his truck to get a huge nail to shore up the frame. There was no way I was going to get to touch the actual cement. Wavy lines were pressed into the grey matter so that the ramp would not become an icy peril in the winter. It was finger-painting on a grand scale.

Paul O'Dwyer drove off in a cloud of dust and the sheep gathered at the gate to watch the cement dry. This prompted a fine story from one of the gang about a cow that had wandered into a fresh cement pad and fallen asleep while the concrete dried around its hooves. I moved the sheep to a far pasture.

Everything was perfect until the work of art was sullied by Groucho the duck that walks like a man and thinks he is a rooster. Groucho was faster than the four men chasing him when he caught sight of his favourite hen standing inside the barn at the edge of the ramp. Duck prints in the concrete added just the right amount of character to what was heralded as "the Boulton pour."

That night I went to the barn to see how things were settling. Concrete looks like concrete even in the moonlight. I thought I would close the barn door and let everything get back to normal.

Then I realized why there had been no ramp to the barn in the first place. The barn door closes sideways on a large sliding hinge, and its bottom was now six inches lower than the cement ramp.

Maybe I would have been better off with a giant bird bath.

Reflections on a Third Eye

IT TOOK ME QUITE A WHILE TO REALIZE THAT I HAD A mark on my forehead. Invisible to the naked eye, it flashed like a beacon when I showed up at any community function remotely affiliated with a walk-a-thon or a pancake breakfast or a bingo for a good cause. It revealed itself to organizers desperately in search of another body to help with hot dog day in the kindergarten class and hospital administrators in need of impartial judges for logo design contests. The third-eye of the volunteer was visited upon me.

From the very first question I asked at my local lamb producers' association meeting, I believe I was looked upon as future fodder. Less than a year later, I was invited to stand for election as the group's secretary. Résumé in hand, I showed up at the meeting wearing a dress rather than my usual blue jeans. After the retiring secretary nominated me, I addressed the group briefly, confessing my shepherdly inexperience but drawing attention to my note-taking abilities. This was greeted with quiet smiles.

There were no other nominees. I served as secretary for six years before I could find another novitiate who bore the mark.

Newcomers to the country are of particular interest to the volunteer sector specifically because they have no history in the community. They have not spent an Arbour Day planting trees beside the river, so they do not recall the year that the Arbour Day planting took place in ankle-high poison ivy. A newcomer can canvas door-to-door raising charitable funds and she will be hearing all of the stories about all of the ailments of the housebound for the first time. New volunteers can suggest things that seasoned volunteers would never dream of making. They can be pardoned for coming up with a craft sale alternative to the fuzzy, imitation poodle, Kleenex box cover that the association's president designed personally a decade ago.

I suspect it was my newness that attracted the attention of the local historical society. A neighbouring township had compiled a local history and it had been a great success. Now it was time for our township to go them one better. Committees had been formed, grants allocated and quotes solicited from printers. Senior citizen historians had been combing the community for old photographs and reminiscences. What they wanted was someone who could help organize the material into a book. I was appointed as editor.

It seemed like something I could handle. Dotting a few i's and crossing a few t's was about all they said they needed. The group calculated that finishing the book would take about eight months. It would be called *Minto*

Memories and launched at the fall fair. The parade float was already in the planning stages. The book's cover would be royal blue with silver lettering. Did I think that was a good idea?

I was given a filing cabinet and boxes filled with family histories and photographs. No one told me that there were almost five hundred historic families in the township. And no one could have known that more than nine hundred photographs would be submitted.

There were family histories that had been generated on computers. Family histories that had been beautifully scripted in calligraphic hand. Family histories stained with gravy and family histories with addenda written on the back of telephone bill envelopes. Special committees formed to gather information on schools, churches, veterans, railways, sports, Women's Institutes and industries. There were poems and maps and stories about sleigh rides in buffalo robes. School children were invited to submit drawings. Little Larry Dean drew a picture of a log cabin, two men on horseback and what appeared to be an outhouse. "The pioneers had no TV so they just played games and sang," he wrote.

Twelve full pages of the book featured pictures of twins and triplets.

Whole meetings were devoted to figuring out who was who in photographs. Tempers flared in debates over who begat whom or who had the first automobile on any given concession. When sensitive subjects arose, committee members would sometimes visit me privately to explain the whole tangled story of the skeleton in the closet and the reason it was going to stay in that closet no matter what so-and-so had to say. That was where being a newcomer helped. The committee could have in-bred the entire township and I would not have known the difference. In the end, it was determined that stories about things such as moonshine stills would be bylined "Totally Anonymous."

It took us two and half years to complete the book.

"Bet you never thought it would take this long," said Mary Seifried, the wife of the committee chairman, as we watched a line-up of book buyers form in the arena after the parade. Mary always brought home-baked cookies to the meetings. I realized how much I was going to miss everyone. What would I have to do now on Monday evenings? Was it possible to have a kitchen table that was not covered with file folders and photocopies of Crown Deeds?

Then I felt a light tap on my shoulder. "We are having a fund-raiser banquet this fall, and we just wondered if you would mind..."

A Barn Is a Barn
Is a Shed, For Truth

ONE OF THE FIRST REALITIES THAT I HAD TO CONFRONT when I moved to the farm was the fact that I did not have a barn. A falling down chicken coop, yes. A barnlike structure sinking into a swamp, yes. But there was no sign of the bulky round-roofed buildings that seem to define the term "farm." This was surely an oversight on my part and one that I realized I would have to rectify before the sheep needed a winter home.

I had one quote from a construction outfit and realized that the cost of building a two-storey barn was significant. The term "pole building" began to have an appealing ring. My neighbour Elmer was of the opinion that building costs could be kept to a minimum by using previously owned materials. He offered to help co-ordinate the scavenging and found that much of the stuff I needed was lying in various yards at various farms that he owned. Soon wagon loads of wood were stacked up in my yard. I learned how to remove previously installed nails with hammer claws, crow bars and combinations thereof. Moose and Elmer dragged huge spruce and cedar poles out of a local pond where they had been curing for some time.

One of the good things about sheep is that their housing requirements are fairly basic. Give them some space in a dry place out of the wind that has plenty of fresh air and they are happy. We settled on a simple rectangular structure with a large sliding door on one side. It was the kind of shape that would be easy to add on to and straightforward to construct. Elmer installed the strategic posts and suggested Mennonite builders to do the framing and finishing. They were private people, he explained. He would tell them what I wanted done. Otherwise, I should not interfere.

When the harvest had ended and I was packing up the scarecrow, two buggies pulled up filled with men named Martin — there were Edwins and Harveys and Sidneys and friends of Ananias Martin. They brought their own hammers and mallets and started right at it. At lunch time, I asked them if they wanted to eat their dinner in the house but the weather was so fine that they opted for the picnic table, divvying out loaves of bread made into hearty sandwiches.

Halfway through the second day, there was a knock at the front door. It was a young Edwin who was acting as assistant to his taller relative, Sidney.

"We were wondering," he began in halting English flavoured with a German accent, "did you want the barn to last for forty years or one hundred?"

This is a question whose strength of character I would ruminate on for many years to come, but at the time I did not hesitate.

"One hundred would be best," I told him. Edwin smiled and nodded his head. I was given a list of building materials to acquire.

Sidney, Edwin and I went shopping for steel siding to put on the building. This meant taking the truck. We loaded into the front seat and Sidney gave me directions. We seemed to traverse every sideroad in the county to get to the place. As we bumped along dirt trails marked "No Winter Maintenance," Edwin and Sidney pointed out various of their relatives' farms. Occasionally, they would say, "That's new," and then they would break into German. Later, I learned there was a direct route to the steel supplier that took about ten minutes, but from the truck Edwin and Sidney could conduct a neighbourhood tour that would take days by buggy. I discovered roads I never knew existed.

Construction dictated the gauge and quantity of steel we would need. The only variable was colour. Edwin, Sidney and I walked past a rainbow of shades until they planted themselves in front of panels of plain galvanized metal. When the salesman calculated the price for coloured steel versus plain steel, the builders Martin gasped audibly.

I paused. Did I need a red and green barn? Would the sheep care if their walls were plain old steel? Would the Mennonites respect me if I proved so spendthrift as to fall prey to installing vanity steel? The salesman seemed to sense my dilemma.

"You can always paint the galvanized after it's weathered a few seasons," he whispered. I ordered the plain steel. Once again, Edwin nodded.

Cold weather was closing in fast. The men agreed to eat at the kitchen table. An offer of hot coffee was welcomed but when I served my potent brew the Martins's eyes bulged. After that, Edwin was designated as the coffee foreperson and I showed him how to make weak coffee. My rudimentary knowledge of German caught me understanding a jocular comment about Edwin being a better woman than the woman. When I nodded at Edwin, the comments stopped abruptly.

Finishing the roof involved the help of Martin children who scaled the steel and pounded nails like pros. My job was passing the nails. No one even asked my name. Finally, one of the bolder boys called down to me, "Do you like this shed for sheep?" and I responded over the rat-tat-tat of hammering with a thumbs up gesture. When the kids left that day, I waved to them and they all raised their mittens in a thumbs up. I had unwittingly corrupted the gesticulation of a generation.

The final touch was installing the sliding barn door. Edwin and Sidney did it by themselves. When they came to the kitchen door to tell me they were finished, a heavy snow had started to fall.

"You tell us if it is not good. Goodbye," said Sidney, handing me the bill solemnly.

"For truth, it is a winter wonderland," I heard Edwin say as they clip-clopped away.

"For truth, it is," said Sidney.

And, for truth, I hope that when the sheep shed celebrates its centennial, someone gives the old building a thumbs up salute — even though the red and green paint is cracked and peeled.

The Last Garage Sale

WHEN I WAS GROWING UP IN THE SUBURBS OUTSIDE OF the major urban centre we rural folks call "the Big Smoke," everyone had a garage. Some were tidy affairs lined with hooks for mounting ladders and garden tools. Some were messy affairs filled with work benches and kids' bicycles and the usual detritus of outgrown toys. Old end tables and couches that might one day find their way to the dream of a cottage could be stacked in the garage, just like yesterday's news. More often than not, there was even room for a station wagon.

No one in the suburbs of my youth would have ever considered dragging the garage dreck onto the front lawn and trying to fob it off on the innocent for a few bucks. In the polite society that played the unspoken game of "my barbecue is bigger than your barbecue," garage contents were as furtively secret as the family treasures that were hidden in the parents' underwear drawers.

Times change. Today the first sighting of a "garage sale" sign is almost as revered as the first robin of spring.

City people are so accustomed to surveying their neighbourhood garage sales and finding the same assortment of rusted TV-tables and bad lamps that they have been compelled to move further afield. Now entire rural towns designate garage sale days and vans filled with urbanites descend in search of quaint, faintly amusing, trinkets from a lifestyle less familiar than the guy next door's.

One person's junk becomes another's obsession. My friend Bette collects waffle irons at garage sales, secondhand stores and auctions. She has a shed full of them. Some with frayed cords, some with rusted bits and some that just need a bit of cleaning up. I have never seen Bette eat a waffle, but that is not her point. She thinks of the old waffle irons as potential gifts for acquaintances and relatives. Reconditioned waffle irons have come to represent her stab at frugality in retirement. And, it makes her happy.

Grandpa Bill and Rick Rooney are another matter. Both grown men, more often than not gainfully employed, they view garage sales as a sort of independent business opportunity. In the world according to Bill and Rooney everything costs a quarter, or it is not worth a ten cents. Up at 5 a.m. on garage sale Saturday, they generally have a route all planned out. If they can, they try to sneak a peak when people are setting up tables the night before. Nothing excites them more than the creak of a virgin garage door opening to reveal its world of wonders.

Most of the stuff they collect in their rounds ends up at Grandpa Bill's, stuffed in the basement or covered with tarpaulins outside. The organization of material is loose. Old books are favoured, along with old signs and lawnmowers that just need a part here or there. "Perfectly good" is their watchphrase.

What Bill and Rooney discovered after years of garage sale haggling is that most people who hold garage sales are so fed up with nickel and diming at the end of the day that they just want whatever is left over to disappear. So, after spending the morning collecting a total of about four dollars worth of "good stuff," Bill and Rooney spend the late afternoon revisiting garage sales and offering to remove the remainder for free, or a quarter.

By fall, the pair have accumulated a mass of garage sale excess that rivals what most rural towns can offer in a weekend. They wait, biding their time through September and October when the garage sale phenomenon starts to wane. By November, most people have packed up their garages for the winter and farm auctions have about come to a standstill. There exists a void in Saturday mornings. It is time for "the last garage sale."

Alex, a local fellow who has a lawn maintenance business, keeps Bill and Rick posted on weather patterns through the Internet. When that one sunny November weekend is headed our way, the tables begin to appear on Bill's lawn and the signs go up on the highway with arrows directing the traffic. Cars line Bill's long lane and families trudge across the frosted lawn for one last fling at a bargain.

At the last garage sale, books are a nickel. A whole carton might go for a quarter, especially if Bill and Rick have already read them. Kids' bikes, playpens, toys and mismatched China pieces end up in car trunks and tucked into back seats. The packrat pals gleefully note that they have sold the same end table three or four years in a row, for a profit of about a dollar in total. One ancient hockey net has made the rounds five times. A bad watercolour that was a bad watercolour in 1992 still sells for a quarter every year. And as long as there are garages, there will always be one more "perfectly good" waffle iron for Bette to add to her collection.

Patrick, He Dead

PATRICK WAS A BEAGLE. HE WAS FULL GROWN WITH floppy spotted ears and paws that seemed disproportionately large in contrast to his snakelike tail. Just a kind of regular beagle, he came to live with my neighbours, the Houstons, some time after the family observed a mourning period for their first family dog, Buford.

It is unlikely, however, that Ken Houston — the patriarch of the clan — will ever stop grieving for Buford. The long-haired, sandy-coloured dog of unknowable breed was a puppy when Ken brought him into the marriage. When "the Buf" finally sighed his last sigh, he was three years older than the eldest adolescent Houston daughter, Amy. Ken buried him in a special spot that only he knows.

Patrick was no Buford, but he managed to develop his own special character and carve his own special place in the affections of the Houston females. Ken's wife, Joy, found the dog pleasant and goofy enough. Amy and her younger sister Angie found it refreshing to have a dog that could keep up with them on a walk. Buford's pace had been rather slow in his latter years.

The fact that Patrick could walk quickly was not missed on Ken or the rest of the folks on the concession. Up at dawn to do his chores in the horse barn, Ken would see the beagle trotting down the road, or crossing it and bounding into a vacant field to check out the groundhog holes.

Dogs that run off their own property are frowned on in the country. Ken knew this very well. Buford had been a stay-at-the-barn, inspect-the-fenceline and go-no-further kind of mutt. Patrick was more like an aborigine called to stroll the neighbourhood by some primordial muse that only he heard. At least, Patrick never seemed to hear Ken when he tried to call him back home. He just wagged his tail when Joy wagged her finger at him for breaching the property line.

Not that Patrick ever caused any harm in the neighbourhood. He was a gentlemanly beagle, not a vagrant. Sometimes he would come up my lane. Dopey and drooling, he would visit my dog's water bowl and take a great slurp on a hot day. Then he would tour whatever tires and trees that held some peculiar fascination for his right leg. He would walk among the chickens without so much as a nip, and he had no inclination to chase sheep. He seemed to like horses but he stayed away from them.

Car tires, truck tires and tree trunks seemed to be the motivating factor behind Patrick's wandering. He liked meeting new people, too.

That weakness for new people proved to be Patrick's downfall. One day, Ken watched as the beagle sauntered along the road beside a young girl from the trailer park-campground down the road. She was probably a summer camper, up with the family to enjoy a few weeks' holiday in a tin can bungalow overlooking a fetid lake, polluted by camper sewage and chemical run-off from the fertilizer ladled on the adjoining golf course. Patrick could have been the highlight of her vacation.

Visiting the trailer park was something everyone in the Houston clan did regularly. As a nurses' aide, Joy went down twice a week in the evenings to replace the Band-Aids on young boys who attended hockey camp. Amy and Angie both worked at "the lodge" changing bedsheets in the few units that operated as a motel for people without tents or trailers. Ken was known to stop by the golf course restaurant for a beer and a burger at lunch time, but he never went back in the evening because of the karaoke machine in the lounge. Ken was never the sort who could stand to watch people humiliate themselves in public.

Joy tried tethering Patrick to a rope on the front lawn, but he would always slip his collar. Not that his collar identified him in any particular way. Ken hid the dog when the township dog licensing servant came up the driveway. When Buford died he still had nine months left to go on his dog licence. No way Ken was going to spend eight dollars on the beagle, even though Buford's nine months were more than a year old.

That summer was a busy one. Rain plagued the haying, so when a good patch of weather came along Ken and the girls worked like fiends to fill the horse barn for winter. Ken is into standardbred racing as a full-time occupation. In some ways, that takes a lot more courage than other types of farming, which at least enjoy the prospect of having a product to sell.

Every decade or so, Ken breeds himself a champion. He still focuses on the bloodlines of Black Mist, a mare who died at twenty-six in 1990. He had sold one of her off-spring for $100,000 — hence the new drive shed and Joy's expanded kitchen. Two of Black Mist's grandnieces were showing some speed, so twice a week he was trucking them around to various racetracks, hoping against hope that someone would make him an offer he could not refuse before a pebble in the hoof or a splinter in a shin bone ended the dream.

Nobody paid too much attention when Patrick disappeared for a few days at a time. Someone would spot him — or at least the tail end of him — sticking out of a groundhog hole. One night he woke Joy up when she heard him off howling in the bush, no doubt stalking the jackrabbits who were claiming the Houston lettuce patch. His food and water were on the front porch. Sometimes there was less there in the morning.

When round, open-faced Angie heard that the dog catcher had been called to take Patrick away from the trailer park, the Houstons realized that no one had seen the beagle for about a week. The odd thing was that everyone who worked at the "recreational complex" knew that Patrick was the Houston dog who lived just up the road, barely a nine-iron shot from the fourteenth hole.

A camper probably called in Wilf Hall without telling anybody. All it would take was a call to the township office and the clerk would have dispatched the legendary dog catcher. Mr. Hall was not a legend because of his skill, but rather because of the lack of it. He was best known for having murdered two dogs in cold blood.

Minto Township had not had much luck with dog catchers. One of the ones before Wilf Hall had been raided by the Humane Society. She lived in an abusive relationship with a town cop, but that was no excuse for the way she managed the puppy mill and menagerie she kept in her barn, which also served as the township dog pound. Cock-a-poos and collies, poodles and spaniels had to lie down in small, dark pens filled with feces. Sometimes dead puppies stayed with their living siblings for days until they were chucked onto the dead pile at the back of the barn. When the Humane Society descended on the place they found that an injured dog who had been taken into the pound had been shot. The bullet was said to have come from the cop's service revolver, which was a no-no.

Wilf Hall heard the job was open and he just applied for it and got it. Nobody asked him a lot of questions about his experience; dog catching being about as simple as it sounds. He was given a copy of the township bylaws, which list regulations pertaining to dogs running at large and licensing requirements. There was even something in there about a township prohibition on keeping meat-eating cats over a certain poundage, marsupials, pachyderms and undesignated odd-toed ungulates.

One of Mr. Hall's early assignments was a report of dogs running at large. The neighbours had called it in; one of the dogs had even taken a nip at them. They were likely from the city. A farmer would not have done such a thing — the rule of thumb being that dogs running at large should be shot and then buried with their collars. Nothing more need be said.

Mr. Hall attended the slightly dilapidated home of the dogs' owner, Wayne Cook, and advised Mr. Cook to restrain the animals and get them proper licences within a week. Mr. Cook dutifully fixed his German Shepherd, Max, and the smaller, excitable English Bull Terrier, Dylan, on long chains next to the house. He was working during the day and he did not make it into the township office to buy the licences that week.

After seven days, Wilf Hall checked and found out the licences had not been purchased. He saw it as a sign of failure to co-operate. Anyone could have seen there was going to be trouble. Mr. Hall was on a mission. He was not quite up to going it alone, however, so he enlisted the aid of the township road superintendent, Neil Murray. Together, the two men road out to the Cook place in Hall's pickup truck, in the middle of a September afternoon. Neil Murray knew every pot-hole on every concession. He had worked for the township for more than twenty years, and he knew just about everything about everybody going back a few generations.

No one was home at Wayne Cook's. Max and Dylan were tied up. They strained at their chains, barking at the two strangers. As their master would admit, he had trained them to "put up a show," but they were friendly to people they knew.

Since the dogs had no licences, Mr. Hall got it into his head that he would impound them. Later he told a court that he thought such action would encourage their owner to "understand the seriousness of the situation with the dogs."

While the road superintendent stood by, Mr. Hall tried to get control of the dogs using a long pole with a rope-snare on the end, but he had never been trained in the use of a rope-snare so it did not work. Instead, he went back to his pickup truck and took out his .22 calibre rifle and shot both Max and Dylan in the head. As he explained it to the court, "I destroyed the dogs for the safety of the people in the neighbourhood."

When Judge H.A. Rice convicted Wilf Hall of unlawfully killing the two chained dogs, he left the matter of restitution up to the civil court. So far as anybody knows Wayne Cook never took the matter any further. Instead, he moved away.

Mr. Hall's lawyer, Ernie McMillan, argued that his client really thought that he had the authority to kill the dogs. He put the blame for that on Minto Township for not bothering to explain the duties, rights and privileges of dog catching under the bylaw, and then not bothering to provide instruction in the craft of actual dog catching. It must have been quite a presentation for Mr. McMillan to make, since his general practice mostly involves real estate transfers, traffic violations and wills.

Wilf Hall was given an absolute discharge, leaving him free to tell the world he has no criminal record so he can enter foreign countries with impunity. But instead of leaving so much as the county, he stayed on as the township dog catcher. At an "in camera" session, the local council voted to keep Mr. Hall on the payroll. They sent him on a two-day dog catcher training course — at the taxpayers' expense. Most of the taxpayers never knew what hit their mill rate, since the case of the canine homicides was scantily reported in the local newspaper.

Ken Houston only knew about Mr. Hall's misadventure because his pal, Mark MacKenzie, sits on the Minto Township council. He also boards a few standardbreds at Ken's. Mark told Ken that he had been the only dissenting vote at the in camera council session. Being a MacKenzie, Mark takes the task of being an elected officer very seriously, even though as a junior member simple mathematics would tell him that he can dissent all he wants and it will not change the way the old guard votes. And, since most of the important political decisions in the township are made in camera where taxpayers are among the great uninvited, there is no podium from which the dissenter might grandstand. Except, of course, for the fact that information about who says what about whom and what to whom at the in camera sessions quickly becomes the talk of the coffee shop as soon as the road superintendent leaves the meeting.

Mark regularly unburdened his angst on Ken over a case of cold ones in the empty box stall where the racing harnesses are stored. Information being a commodity, these sessions served to bond the two men, and Ken rather liked having a friend in "high places." Mark even managed to have Ken appointed to the arena board, which added $300 a year to the Houston coffers and allowed Ken to have some say in the management of the ice hockey food booth. It also meant that Mark had someone to talk to at the annual township employees' Christmas party.

High places could not help Patrick. Ken asked Mark to make inquiries, and Mark determined that the unlicensed beagle had been duly dispatched by Wilf Hall exactly three days after he was impounded. Everything was done in accordance with the bylaws.

Of the two girls, the youngest, Angie, was the most upset. Ken figured she was misty-eyed for about a day. Amy, the more analytical of the two, just could not figure out why somebody had not said something before calling in the dog catcher. Joy shrugged and threw out the stale dog food that was collecting flies on the porch. She grew up in the country. When a dog runs, something like this is bound to happen.

Mark bought the Miller High Life the next time he saw Ken. They disposed of it in one afternoon, while Mark expounded on his theory of events. At least one citizen had written a letter opposing the retention of Mr. Hall's services and suggesting that the township dock a day's pay from Neil Murray, who had been neglecting his duties as road superintendent by attending the execution of Wayne Cook's companion animals. But Patrick was still dead.

Privately, Ken has confessed that the beagle was never much of a dog. He caused more trouble than his feed was worth and he was always chasing after the tractor tires, trying to bite them, or pee on them, or just bark at them because they were in motion. Sure, he spent a lot of time around groundhog holes, but there was never any evidence that he ever caught one. Even worse, when a friend of Joy's employed Patrick as a beagle stud, he failed. In Ken's world, where a consignor pays big fees based on the delivery of a "live foal," Patrick was nothing less than totally useless — an embarrassment to boot.

The other Houstons tried to get Ken to reclaim the

body so Patrick could at least have a proper burial, but Ken already had closure.

"I'm not going to pluck him out of that pile they've probably got stacked and ready for the bulldozer," he said. "He'll go with the rest into that Rwanda-style mass grave, and no more talk about it."

Only Ken knows where Buford is buried and only Ken can visit with him. A dog can be a sacred trust, a friend that stays in the heart long after its heart stops beating. But as for Patrick, he dead.

A Hands-On Legend

LEGEND HAS IT THAT COUNTRY FOLK ARE BY NATURE A
more decent and honest lot than their urban cousins. It is
a pleasant enough legend, and I have found it can be
worked to one's advantage. I used it once when I was
researching the wool industry at a reference library in the
city. All I wanted to do was photocopy an arcane article
about felt-making in Great Britain, which I found in an
obscure sheep journal.

"Sorry the photocopier is broken and we do not allow
materials to be removed from this department," the
library technician told me. "People steal things like this all
the time. You will just have to come back tomorrow, or
take notes."

I explained that this would be impossible, since I was
from out of town. Notes were just not feasible since the
text in question was impenetrably mathematical. The
wool washing instructions alone dealt with temperatures
and tonnage and soap to litre ratios that would take me an
entire winter to analyze. Then I waved the article in front

of her as evidence and asked if I could please use the working photocopier in the adjoining department.

"You in the clothing business?" she asked with some suspicion, her tweedy eyes narrowing as she examined the object of my desire.

"Oh, no, no, nothing like that," I said. "I'm a farmer. I raise sheep. That's why I'm reading up on wool."

She eyed me with even more suspicion. I guess I had "warshed up real good," as they say in the country. At least, I did not smell like a sheep. My polished leather boots bore no trace of the barnyard and the neat folds of my skirt showed no signs of recent tumbling in the hay. I had no alternative but to produce my hands as proof positive of my profession.

Mine have always been active rather than elegant hands. No square French manicures for these fingernails. What kind of psychotic lambing midwife would subject her trusting ewes to long nails of any shape? And since you cannot pour hot water on frozen taps while wearing unwieldy mittens, the texture of the surrounding flesh becomes somewhat roughened in rough weather. My hands are only truly soft when the lanolin in the sheared sheep's wool has drenched them in smoothing oil. Unfortunately, that only happens one day of the year and there is plenty of sheep by-product that comes with the lanolin.

A scar marks the right palm where a horse inadvertently kicked me. Another ragged mark distinguishes a different horse who mistook my left thumb for a carrot. Various bumps and gnarls come from long-forgotten incidents that involve everything from scrappy chickens who refused to surrender their eggs to hammers that eluded nails. All ten digits are in working order, however, and working is what they reveal.

"Goodness, you *must* be a farmer," said the clerk, widening her eyes and lowering her chin. To brighten the light bulb that was dawning over her head, I produced a photograph of a newborn lamb that I carry in my wallet like a doting parent.

"I promise to return the magazine right away," I assured her in a whisper appropriate to the location.

"You know, I believe you," she said in the same tone that teachers use on errant students to whom they are giving one last chance before calling for parental intervention.

I scurried over to the next department and inserted my quarter. Two minutes later, I was back at her desk replacing the well-travelled document. The library technician smiled at me as though I had sprinkled her with fairy dust.

It might not work with automated bank machines, but there are times when belonging to a profession that has decency and honesty as its legend can sure come in handy.

Winter

Flannelette Dreams

THE FIRST DAY OF WINTER ON THE FARM IS THE DAY that I put flannelette sheets on the bed. Usually, it is also the first night that snow blankets the ground and stays there. It is the night when the one garden hose that escaped the autumn garden clean-up freezes into place until spring.

That first lasting snow brings with it the mixed emotions that challenge everyone who lives with the stuff. Something about it recalls the rapture of childhood excitement over being able to make snowballs any time you want, building snowmen and designing snow forts. It also recalls the wind-whipped days, windshields blinded by a cataclysm of falling flakes and sludge falling from encrusted boots onto so-called draining trays by the front door.

And then there are the flannelette sheets. To me, they are second only to homemade stew with dumplings as a cure for any winter day. There is an air of comfort about flannelette sheets that makes you feel that the misery of the weather cannot get you. And, of course, if you sleep in the nude, flannelette sheets are mandatory in any house that takes on a chill at night.

The question then becomes: what has happened to flannelette sheets in modern times? The flannelette of my childhood seemed so much thicker, so much more cuddly. Every winter for years, they were the same flannelette sheets as always — plain white, trimmed only with a line of pink and blue at the top. They were washed a zillion times in the same washing machine, by the same mother, year after year, and they always felt the same. Smooth.

However, the flannelette sheets I have acquired as an adult are not like those of my youth. Granted they do come in a riot of colours to mix and match and co-ordinate with nude, or whatever colour you sleep in. These new-fangled flannelette sheets start out just grand but after a few washings they start to fizzle into a fuzzy-nubbed surface. I think the formal word is "pilling." The principle is the same one that applies to certain sweaters, which develop pesky "pills" of wool at the worn bits around the neck and at the wrists. In between the fuzzy bits on the sheets, the layer of flannelette is skimp and limp, so you have to try to wrap yourself in the fuzzy bits to get that feeling of flannelette security.

Complaining about the declining quality of flannelette gets you absolutely nowhere. I know, I tried.

"You can see that the flannelette is all fuzzy right here," I said to the clerk in the "major retail shopping store," where I had purchased a set of cornflower blue flannelette sheets. "In fact, you can see it quite clearly because the fuzzy bits are still cornflower blue, while the unfuzzy bits are more of an azure blue."

"Well, they *are* a year old," sniffed the clerk, without even bothering to touch the freshly laundered sheet I had trucked all the way to the big city, lugged from a parking lot across four intersections and hauled up four escalators. Instead of sympathizing with me or even apologizing for the poor quality of the product, this whippet-thin clerk with skin the texture of 200-thread percale and attitude worthy of a bank manager was trying to make *me* feel like some sort of slob because my sheets went fuzzy halfway through the winter.

So I asked to see the linen supervisor, thinking that perhaps I would find satisfaction with a more mature individual who understood the true nature of flannelette.

"How did you wash this," was the first question that emerged from the lips of a thirty-something supervisor. I noticed that he had pills on the wrists of his cardigan.

This was obviously a trick question; but before I could pick the lint out of my thoughts, the truth was on the table.

"Warm water, tumble dry," I sputtered.

"Bleach?" he asked, twisting the word as though anyone so stupid as to add bleach to a load of laundry had the personality potential to poison the entire city water supply.

"No, never," I responded, perhaps too quickly to make even the truth believable. I stuck my chin out to emphasize my point.

Stymied but unmoved, the supervisor deigned to actually touch the fuzzy sheet, which I thought would be a defining moment.

"Well, it *goes* like this when you use it" he said, stroking the sheet as though it were a sick puppy. Then he started to leave.

"But you're supposed to use it, that's why you buy it and now it's all fuzzy and my mother's flannelette was never fuzzy and it's just not the same…" or words to that effect burbled out of me as he walked away.

"Sorry," was all he said as he headed for the duvet aisle and the perfect oblivion of goose down.

All the way home, I kept thinking of snappy retorts and clever rebuttals to arguments that had never been made. I even contemplated writing a letter to the store's president suggesting he inspect his linen department employees for wrist pills, because if they are satisfied wearing pilly clothes, they surely do not give a yahoo about selling flannelette that goes fuzzy after a few washings.

A few days later, I went to the big pre-Christmas sale at my local Stedman's store. Stedmans is like a small-scale Wal-Mart, except that you are likely to find the owner working the floor. You can find almost anything in Stedmans from bikini underwear to clothes pegs and shower curtains. The pre-Christmas sale is usually a jumble of stuff that has been stacked up in the storeroom for longer than anyone can remember.

That is where I found my "real" flannelette sheets. On the bottom shelf of the linen aisle, there was a clear plastic bag with a set of white sheets trimmed with pink and blue. Nothing fancy marked them, no designer label, no nothing. Ruth, the owner, told me she found them in a box in the back room and that they must have been left by the previous owner. Heck, she even found a carton of Pet Rocks back there. I opted to buy the flannelette sheets.

After going through the washing machine ten times, those sheets are still smooth. They tumble dry into fluffy perfection. One touch of them makes you a nighttime nudist for the whole winter.

When I close my eyes at night and briefly ponder ways of extricating the garden hose from its frozen resting place, the flannelette sheets take hold and lull me into dreams that are as cuddly as a childhood memory.

The Moment of Realization

In the country, community is a loosely defined term that starts with family and tends to spread itself around through a network of marriages, friendships and other relationships. When a stranger enters that environment, there is an uneasiness on both sides that only time and curiosity and the same sort of ritual sniffing that dogs partake of can overcome.

I do not know exactly when the community I live in accepted me as part of its fabric, but there was one epiphanic moment when I knew that I was home.

It happened a few years after I moved to the farm. I was still struggling to figure out who was who and what was where in my immediate neighbourhood. Making friends was not easy without the social life of a job, and so many things always seemed such a long drive away. In my first year I signed up for a water aerobics class a full township away. Everyone in my class was a good quarter-century older than I was and the sessions were more like Beginners Whirlpool than exercise. No one would talk to me because I was young enough to be their daughter, but I was nobody's daughter and I was from "away."

I mentioned this to my neighbour Gerry one day. Geraldine is a private sort of woman. Her husband, Jack, had been blowing the snow out of the lane for two full years before we met and discovered we were related. They had stopped in for Christmas tea and Gerry kept saying there was something awfully familiar about me. But they were pig farmers and they hardly ever went to the city, so we could not figure out what sort of sherry Gerry was sipping. But when she got home, Gerry found me in the family photo album.

I was about ten years old and I was standing in a cemetery. It turned out that my paternal grandfather, Harry, had married Jack's widowed mother, Edith, in their Golden Years. They had lived briefly in the town of Mount Forest until Edith's death. I remembered Granddad's wedding to a woman who smelled of lavender, and I sort of recalled driving for endless hours to visit them in a little town with one grocery store where people dressed in black and tied up their horses and buggies in the parking lot. All I recalled about the funeral was thinking it quite strange that anyone would want to take pictures, but I did not mention that.

Somehow, that vague connection made me close to being family. Gerry asked me if I would like to join the women's bowling league.

"Long as you don't mind losing, that is," she said.

Well, I never thought that I would find myself wearing shoes previously worn by others, but Wednesday afternoon at the bowling alley turned out to be a hoot.

Our team was the Try Hards — and we did — but no one took it seriously. We played the five-pin game, not because we thought the big balls were for men, but rather because it was easier. There were young mothers playing with their mothers, middle-agers playing with their high school chums and enough carbonated oldsters to keep things lively.

I stayed quiet the first half of the year, conversation being difficult at best in a bowling alley. But I picked up shreds of conversation and I learned about things that were going on — difficult births, mumps in the Grade Five class, anniversary socials for people celebrating fifty years of wedlock even though they had not spoken to each other for a decade — that sort of thing.

Then my doctor called me one Wednesday morning and confirmed my worst fears. I would need to have surgery for the removal of an early form of cancer.

"No big deal," my doctor said, "two or three days in hospital. You'll be back for Christmas."

So I had to tell my team that I would not be attending the bowling league Christmas party. They already knew something was wrong because I did not do a little dance when I bowled a strike. And they agreed with me that the C word was a very big deal, no matter how nascent. I had hugs and promises that they would freeze me a piece of cake.

The dawn of the day I was to go into the hospital was as grim as my mood. Worse, when I turned on the water tap, there was nothing but a sputter of air. My step-uncle Jack was blowing the snow from the lane when he spotted me leaving the shed where the well pump lives.

"Trouble?" he asked. I told him there was and he had a look.

Diagnosis: "Pipe's broke underground somewhere between the pump and the house. She's going to have to be dug up and replaced. Pipe'll be five or six feet down."

I had six hours to get it done, if I could find a plumber who was available four days before Christmas. And a backhoe operator and an electrician and anyone else who might be needed.

I started with the plumber. Busy signals, nothing but busy signals. When I finally got through and stammered out my explanation of things as I understood them, he asked me again, "And your name is?"

He repeated it slowly as I spelled it out. Then I heard a familiar voice in the background. It was his wife, the shyest Try Hard on the team, but I could hear her bellowing.

"You get out there right now, Marsha needs to have water, today, man." Then she came on the line and in her shy voice said, "Don't worry, he's coming right now."

Uncle Jack called to say that he was on his way over to Elmer's to help boost the backhoe. My next call was to Clarence the electrician, but he was already en route, courtesy of his wife Helen, the strikes-and-spares queen of the Try Hards. Word was spreading through the bowling league faster than a greased gutter ball.

Trucks and machinery started rolling up the laneway. There were people I knew and people I had never seen before. There were Mennonites with their lunches neatly packed in six-quart baskets and ladies carrying industrial-sized coffee percolators. Once the backhoe broke the frozen ground, a trench half as long as a hockey rink snaked from the house to the little metal shed housing the pump. Men jumped in and the shovel work began. It looked like a scene out of World War I.

By the time I left for the bus, a party atmosphere had taken hold. Kids were ferrying coffee to the workers and women were making sandwiches in an assembly line. I stood at the edge of the trench and shouted my thanks. Ken "the Hooter" Houston looked up at me, grinning, with mud glued to the stubble of his beard.

"And I thought I was just coming over to throw a few bales of hay at the sheep while you were off galavantin' in the big smoke," he shouted.

"Git, girl," said Clarence. "If you don't make that bus, Helen will have my hide."

I returned to the farm two days later. The doctor was right, no big deal. On the kitchen table I found bowls of nuts and candies. Elmer's wife, Betty, sent a decorated fruit basket with a bottle of ginger ale wrapped in foil. Under the sheep fridge magnet, there were instructions about casseroles and pies in the freezer. Someone had tied a big red bow around the kitchen tap.

The note said, "We always try harder. Welcome home."

Don't Wait Until Dark

LIVING IN THE COUNTRY DURING THE WINTER ALSO means living in a state of constant preparedness. One toque, one scarf, one set of mitts is never enough. There always has to be back-up that is accessible — and dry. On a really ugly, soggy-snow day this can mean as many as three full changes of clothing, right down to the long johns. After a while, you start to feel like a giant baby.

Trucks and machinery need to have jumper cables and battery chargers at the ready. Logging chains become a standard piece of equipment to carry around in case someone needs a tow. And a big margarine bucket full of wood ashes comes in awfully handy when the old tires start spinning on ice. As long as there is room in the back of the truck for the dog and the groceries, you know that you have not overdone it. I even find that the dog enjoys resting her head on the ancient Sesame Street sleeping bag I keep rolled up behind the truck seat — just in case.

Better to err on the side of preparedness is also true in the farm house, particularly when it comes to provisions and batteries. I have never been through a winter without at least one sustained power failure that threatens to wreak havoc on everything except the contents of the freezer.

The power usually fails after dark without warning. It never happens at a convenient time. For instance, one minute you are standing in the shower, beginning to rinse the shampoo out of your hair and, bingo, all of a sudden the water stops flowing and you are in the dark dripping bubbles. So you stumble carefully out and begin reaching for the towels that should be handy and you end up wrapping your head in the clean sweatshirt you brought to change into. A hand towel is usually the only thing that seems available for dabbing the remaining wet bits.

First errors aside, even the most lowly apprentice in the business of managing a power outage learns that at least one flashlight must always be stored in a hallowed place where it can be found without mishap. It should not be buried underneath the screwdrivers in the third drawer down in the kitchen. It should not be mounted on a wall with kitchen pots and pans, whose handles could be confused leaving you trying to find a switch on a wok in the dark. It should not be left anywhere near the television gizmo which is chronically missing in action. Instead, at least one flashlight with working batteries should be mounted permanently somewhere convenient to available candlesticks and communications devices — say above, below or beside the telephone in the kitchen, provided said telephone is not a travelling model.

This is all well and good, but unless one retains the control learned in military or reform school, it is difficult to enforce. So I always try to make sure that I know where last summer's barbecue lighter is situated, since it is not prone to temporary borrowing and provides just enough light to find a candle and light it.

I always keep three candles on the kitchen table. It looks kind of romantic, as though every dinner could be a candlelit rendezvous. Once I have them lit, visual sanity can prevail and permit a search for additional sources of light.

Living with power failures also makes you into a flashlight fanatic. Not for the little, two D-cell models, either. I like those flashlights that have snaky cords that you can wrap around things. I have flashlights with long incandescent bulbs that you can hang from coffee-cup hooks. If I need to light up the barnyard, there is a halogen light that plugs into the truck cigarette lighter and floods the yard like a movie set.

There are portable flashlights you can strap to your head, and mini-flashlights that you can attach to reading material. And it never hurts to keep a strand of battery-operated Christmas lights handy for general ambiance. One of my summer-use flashlights even has a built-in bug zapper. If you sit close enough to it, no creepy-crawly, winged things can get you.

Once you have light, ascertaining the magnitude of the hydro failure becomes a priority. Neighbours call neighbours, always with some trepidation since there is always the possibility that the Hydro Grinch has decided that the "cheque-that-is-in-the-mail" is long overdue, so they have arbitrarily pulled the plug. Anytime such an outrage occurs, there is plenty of shed talk about solar power and harnessing the energy of the underground springs to generate our own power and watch the hydro meters run backward for a while.

When a local outage is confirmed, I do what all my neighbours do. We head outside to see if we can spot the local "town" lights glowing in the distant sky. If there are no lights in town, it could be a long outage. The prospect of a long outage seems to have a direct effect on the bladder, which causes a panic in lavatories all over the county.

You see, in the country your water generally comes from a well, and the pump that brings that water to the house (and the loo) is powered by electricity. Hence, a long outage means that if you are caught in mid-shampoo that shampoo is going to harden dry before you can get it rinsed and that one flush that is left in the toilet has got to count.

Everyone tries calling the hydro company, but there is absolutely no point since the lines are always jammed. If you ever do manage to get a live voice on the other end of the line, all you will learn is that "trucks have been dispatched." You will never be told why trucks are needed or where they have been dispatched to or from. Apparently, the idea that there are "trucks" out there is somehow supposed to be a comfort while you slowly freeze and starve in the dark.

Large farming operations often have gas-powered generators to keep things going. Newborn piglets do not have much except the hair on their chiny chin chins to keep them warm, so heat lamps are essential.

Cooped-up chickens need warmth and light to keep their egg production to the maximum. And anyone incubating thousand dollar ostrich eggs wants to keep those giant babies nice and warm.

But sheep do not fret much about hydro, and simple shepherds like me can usually manage in the dark for a few hours until the trucks work their magic.

This is where a wood-burning stove comes in handy. Candles, oil lamps and the crackle and glow from a wood stove create a homespun atmosphere. Until you find the batteries to fire up the transistor radio, it is about as close as you can get to life in pioneer times.

A good iron pot or frying pan is all you need to create a storm-stayed evening meal — canned corned beef with home fries, and scrambled eggs with a tin of baked beans. Something about it feels like chuckwagon swill.

Once you get into the spirit of a power failure, it does not seem like a failure at all. Without the use of a television and a VCR, conversation picks up. Half-read books find their way to the best lit spot in the house and the lovely tradition of reading makes a comeback. Neighbours phone neighbours with outage updates and rumours. If a hydro truck is spotted on the road, it is news that is passed from lip to ear without virtue of a web site.

The hydro usually comes on halfway through some intensely pleasurable, after dinner outage diversion. Suddenly candles seem redundant. Overhead lights glare and digital clocks flash impatiently while five CDs try playing at once. Immediately, there is a scramble to turn things off that were left on and to turn things on that were turned off.

With each outage, a new instruction in "preparedness" presents itself. One year it may be a reminder to stock a few gallon jugs of water in the basement so that toilet flushing can be managed without trauma. Another year it may be a reminder to keep a manual can opener in stock because fancy electric ones will not open a tin of beans during an outage. Maintaining a stockpile of batteries starts to become as automatic as drying your toque.

Of Christmas Trees
and Memories

WHEN I FIRST MOVED TO THE FARM, THERE WAS A twenty-acre field that had been planted with white pine and spruce trees in neat rows. They were only about three feet tall, and it was hard to see them at times because leafy stands of Queen Anne's lace and Canada thistle could dwarf them. So that first Christmas, I scouted the fence row until I found a scraggly wild pine that was taller than me.

It took a few years, but the sheep managed to graze their way through the evergreen rows and nibble out the weeds, fertilizing as they went. There were great advantages to this, since I was teaching a young horse to neck-rein Western style and rows of trees were a natural training arena.

In the spring, the horse and I would wind our way through every other row of trees. Along the way, I would "candle" some of the trees, grabbing the shiny new growth at the end of the boughs and twisting off the soft evergreen ends so that the following year the new growth would be bushy — like a Christmas tree.

After a few years, the trees started growing grandly — tens of thousands of them. The Kinsmen and the Boy Scouts took hundreds off my hands, thinning them as they needed to be and raising money for their projects by selling them at supermarket lots. Neighbours, friends, church groups and passers-by drove up the lane and scouted the field for the perfect tree.

Still, there was always one man who came out every year with his little grandson and they would trudge off — hatchet in hand — to find a tree. But they could never seem to find one that suited them, so they packed up and left.

The problem is that Christmas trees that have not been picked for Christmas keep growing. So after almost twenty years on the farm, I find myself with a wondrous field of two- and three-storey-tall trees which looks more like Temagami than a neatly tended Christmas tree plantation.

People still slog through the bush looking for little ones. Sometimes they find one. And sometimes they let the Paul Bunyan in them come out and cut down a huge tree taking only the topmost part. Come spring, I always have a pile of Christmas tree bottoms to shred into wood chips for the garden.

I can always find a tree that suits me, even if it needs a bit of trimming. It might take days, but the horse and I will wander through the field dodging branches until one particular conifer catches our eye. Sometimes the sheep follow us, for no apparent reason other than curiosity. The final tree is always impossibly big, majestic, round on all sides — and heavy as all get out to drag through the snow.

Years ago, the smaller trees could come through the front door of the house and be manoeuvred into position against the fifteen-foot-high brick walls of the living room. But as the trees grew, so did the dilemma of getting the tree through the door.

In recent years, the logistics have become impossible. So I have taken to bringing the tree into the house through the back way. This painstaking exercise involves removing an entire picture window and balancing the tree on a picnic table before it is gradually inserted and propped upright through a series of ropes and human willpower.

I was contemplating the calories this would burn up when a city friend called to ask how things were going. Nancy and her husband, Geoff, have three young children and a small house. The idea of such a huge tree seemed fantastical.

"How on earth do you decorate it?" she asked.

So I told her about using the extension ladder to install the star at the top. The lights, all 550 of them, sort of drape over the top and all the way down, followed by the ornaments. A collection of antiques, kitsch and baubles that all seem to have a memory behind them are hooked on at random, like the icicles that add the final shimmer. Then I offered the notion that I might not do it again. Maybe, I thought, it was time to give the Boy Scouts and the Kinsmen their chance to sell me a little tree.

Perhaps, I sounded weary. Perhaps, I was thinking about the way the hydro meter would start spinning around as soon as I plugged the tree lights in. Or perhaps, I had forgotten how wondrous a Christmas tree can be. Nancy with the laughing eyes would hear none of that. Her kids had never had a big tree to decorate. They could be the ornament elves. Together, we agreed we would lead the horse and the sheep into the forest and see what we could find.

I rearranged the furniture, so that a whole third of the room was ready to be covered in tree. Boxes of ornaments lined one wall, although I always know the exact location of the purple glass balls that my Aunt Jean gave me. They were wrapped in tissue right above the hanging musical Elvis. The 1993 World Series Blue Jays commemorative ornament was mixed in with ceramic Santa Clauses, shiny balls, plastic apples and the wooden sled ornament on which I painted the name "Rosebud." I love the stuffed penguins that have to be wired to each branch, and Snow White and her Seven Dwarfs — and even the Miss Piggy ornament that I bought on sale at the drug store.

There is nothing Martha-Stewart-correct about my Christmas tree, but it is the kind of tree that grows on you. The kids — Aurora, Olivia and Anna — swarmed the branches, hooking on ornaments and reaching deep into the tree to hide painted pine cones. All of the candy canes were placed within easy child reach. It was their tree, too, and that made it the best tree of all.

A few days after the tree decorating, a teenaged boy came to the door. Something about him looked awfully familiar. He told me that he used to come to the farm when he was a kid, with his grandfather. They were the pair who could never find a Christmas tree. He laughed with me over that one.

His grandfather was dead now, the young man explained. And the reason that they never cut down a tree was that his grandmother had terrible allergies. Now she was gone, too.

"Could I take a walk through the trees?" he asked. And that was all right with me.

I watched him walk off into the forest of Christmases past to commune with his memories, and I realized that the gift of a grandfather — of time spent in the woods, out of the pure spirit of caring — was a larger and brighter memory than any Christmas tree could ever be.

Deep Ditch Bambi

THERE IS A SIGN ON THE ROADWAY WARNING, "THIS Road Is Used By Horse-Drawn Buggies."

That is a courtesy to the Mennonite community, who travel the route regularly to get to town. The problem is that it also attracts warm-weather tourists who sometimes tour the road trying to get a look at the "buggy people." It can be kind of embarrassing for all concerned.

One sign we could use on the road is a warning that the entire route is a deer crossing in winter.

At dawn and dusk, the deer are on the move. I know that they have a path through the wildest part of my forest. It comes out near the mailbox. I have watched them pause there, before they fade back into the forest like grey-brown ghosts.

Sometimes I will be out walking with the dog and she will get a whiff of them and take off on a tear. Not to worry, in snow she is not even fast enough to catch a three-legged groundhog. Often, there is no warning at all. A rustle through the trees is followed by the twang of a fence wire as the deer bound over it. I like knowing that the deer are out there. The problem is they do not know how to cross a road, or when.

Almost every week, the local newspaper reports some sort of confrontation between a deer and a vehicle. Like rabbits, deer will freeze when they are caught in head-lights. On slick roads, a sudden stop can become a dough-nut that leads straight into the ditch.

If the deer runs off before this happens, the ditch is still a danger. Where one white-tail crosses, more are sure to follow. Many times, I have watched one, two, three cross safely well in advance of an oncoming car, only to have a fourth scared young doe leap out of the ditch at the last minute, raising everyone's blood pressure.

In blinding snow, the phenomenon becomes particu-larly heart-stopping. I was rounding the corner on the final few hundred feet of a messy drive home, when I checked the passenger window and saw the haunting fig-ure of a big buck barrelling in my direction to avoid a snowmobile that was closing in on him.

Velvet nose, frightened eyes, a swirl of antlers and snowflakes and he was gone. I cannot say which of us was more shaken by the experience. Windshields and antlers can be a nasty combination.

I guess driving a horse and buggy might give me more time to watch for the warning signs of wildlife at the road's edge. Certainly, if I tried to make the trip to town on a throbbing snowmobile, I would be hard-pressed to see anything except the occasional backside of a deer. There must be an in-between ground that we can all live with so that Bambi does not become a road warrior, or a road kill.

Deep in the forest, there is a spot where I know that deer gather. It is called "yarding up," and you can tell that they have been there by the flattened snow, the tracks and the droppings.

I can understand why they like the spot. The place is hard to find, but it is sheltered. When the sun filters through, the dapple of light creates all sorts of shadows to hide in.

I do not want to alter the course of nature, but I also have no desire to collide with it. So, I put salt licks in the deer yard. That way, the deer do not have to scavenge for whatever tasty minerals might be lurking in the sand that is occasionally laid on the roadway. Deer prefer the small, sweeter white licks that feedstores sell for bunnies. Some stores even have elaborate apple-flavoured concoctions for deer. With great difficulty, the Moose and I managed to role a big bale of hay close to the path that the deer take to the yard, but far out of sight.

I never expect the deer to stay there all winter without moving, and I never let down my guard when I am driving. Occasionally, I find some roadside evidence of a path that they frequent. When I hear a giant tree creak in the forest, I imagine some buck is rubbing against it. At night, I search the fenceline for the glow of their emerald eyes in the barnyard lights.

When spring comes, and the tourists start stalking the Mennonites in their buggies, the deer will have vanished from the roadways. They will become grazing silhouettes on the fringe of the forest — almost imperceptible, almost back to the wilderness.

Smoke Gets in Your Eyes

ON CHRISTMAS EVE, I WOULD DESPERATELY LIKE TO order in Chinese food the way my parents used to do when I was a kid. But you cannot do that in the country, so I get out the wonton wrappers and soy sauce and try for a reasonable facsimile. It is a tradition, although one year it nearly went by the wayside. That year I was lucky to have a household.

On a cold and clear night a few weeks before Christmas, the house almost burned down. It was one of those crisp, starry December nights without any wind to blow the snow. Chores were done and dinner was waiting to be made.

Old brick houses hold a lot of heat, and I plunked a few pieces of cedar beneath a maple log to rekindle the fire in the wood stove. There was time, it seemed, for me to write a long overdue letter to a friend before I started peeling potatoes.

I headed upstairs to the "room of my own" where the computer hums and the books overflow in piles. Pictures on the wall range from old jazz musicians to navigational charts of bodies of waters that I am unlikely to ever navigate, but would like to.

By the fifth step, I knew there was trouble. Farming develops an uncanny sense of smell — a nose tuned to sensibilities of cured hay, or the sickly smell that can come from either end of an animal that is not feeling right.

I smelled smoke, but did not see it, until I opened the closed door of the guest bedroom. It billowed out at me in the darkened hallway, an acrid sheet that hurt my eyes and sent the smoke alarm into a hyper wail.

Peering into the room, I could not see anything ablaze, only yellowish smoke. In a gesture of self-preservation that was almost primeval, I grabbed the brand new, two-piece dress I had laid out on the guest bed in preparation for the annual meeting of the Proton Township Federation of Agriculture where I was scheduled to speak the next evening. Then I slammed the door shut and ran down the stairs.

I have played out this drill in my mind before, but I had no idea how effective it would be. By the placement of the smoke, the only conclusion was "chimney fire," a fact that I calmly announced to the Moose.

He placed the emergency call, while I sealed the wood stove, to avoid feeding oxygen into the chimney. Suddenly, I was able to assemble the boots, scarves and gloves that I never seem able to find otherwise. We clambered into them to get a look at what was going on outside the house.

The century-old chimney pokes out of the second-storey roof, above the guest bedroom. Big red embers and flames were shooting out of it. I turned on the Christmas lights that circle a cedar tree on that side of the house, and we watched the sparks landing and dying on a cover of ice and snow. The residual of a blizzard I had cursed a few days before was protecting the roof over my head.

The smoke had not spread, so I ran upstairs on a mission that I knew would have to be fast. Memories are scattered all over the house, but I keep the photo albums in one big drawer of the hall cupboard. I had never realized how many there were or how much each one meant until I started tossing them into a laundry hamper.

Then I scurried downstairs, knowing I could not return. When I passed the guest room door, smoke was seeping from the bottom. I stuffed a pair of long johns under it to stem the tide. The back of the door was cool. A good sign I thought, as I visualized the room — the apple doll scrunched on the night table and the pine armoire stacked with summer clothes. Against the north wall lay the spool bed on which so many friends say they got their best night's sleep. At the end of it was the quilt with twelve ladies holding parasols that my Grandmother made out of scraps and pieces of clothes I wore when I was a little girl.

The Moose was looking worried when I came down with my booty of memories. Everything seemed to be moving in slow motion, except the crackle and snapping sounds in the chimney. We scooped the usual clutter from the hallway into the hamper to clear the path for the firemen and put the ungainly haul in the back of the truck for safekeeping.

Animals sense when something is up. The sheep and

horses had left the barn and gathered at the fenceline to quietly observe the odd activity. Even Diva Dog accepted her truck-seat assignment with unusual dignity.

In short shrift, an emergency van and two fire trucks were in the lane, along with my neighbour, Joy, and her daughters. When anything with a siren blaring roars down a country road, you can bet everyone pays attention. Joy heard the commotion and went outside to see what was happening. Sure enough, above the tall trees that surround my place, she could see black smoke covering the stars.

While the firemen went about the business of spreading tarpaulins around the wood stove and investigating the upstairs nightmare, Joy, Angie, Amy and I shuffled boxes of files and computer disks outside. Moose disconnected the "brain" of his computer and ferried it to safety.

Upstairs, in the room next to the fire site, sat my own computer and its precious, helpless brain where my own manuscripts and mangled thoughts awaited possible incineration. I tried not to think about that.

Outside, the firemen were going swiftly about their business. Ladders helped them scale the roof, but the blessed protective blanket of snow and ice did not make getting to the top of the chimney easy. When I saw them unravelling the water hose and adjusting gauges on the pump truck, a wave of horror hit me. For the first time, I noticed that some of the men were wearing what looked like oxygen masks as they entered the house. This was not a movie, the danger was real.

In the kitchen, where there was surprisingly little smoke, I recognized Len, the man who runs the feed mill at the local Co-Op store. He was spreading a huge tarp over the cluttered kitchen table.

"Anything else we should cover, Marsha?" he asked.

In my heightened state, I noticed two things — one was the operative word "cover," and the other was the easy, soothing way that he said my name. These were not unknown firemen. Underneath their masks and black and yellow suits — these were my neighbours, people whom I had seen cheering the home team at the hockey arena and people whose houses, farms and children I knew by sight.

When you are facing the potential loss of all of your "stuff," identifying one thing as "special" is hard, but I asked Len if it would be possible to throw something over the old wooden cabinet in the kitchen corner. It conjured visions of the day we discovered it in the dusty corner of an old curiosity shop. Then there was the struggle to get it through the front door and the joyful decision to leave it as we found it, with the colourful green and orange paint that its Ukrainian pioneer builders had given it.

While Len pondered the logistics, I started stuffing knickknacks and old salt and pepper shakers from the shelves into my purse for safekeeping. When I found myself carefully charting a course across the kitchen floor carrying a martini glass that holds a collection of hand-blown glass swizzle sticks bought at an auction years ago, I knew I was losing my composure.

Apparently, at that very surreal moment the chimney fire bowed to the assorted flame retardants and suffocation efforts of the heroes upstairs. Amy whispered in my ear that she heard one of the firemen say he did not think they would need water. An hour later, it was over.

Len and the men were cautious, they checked the attic and the roof many times before they were satisfied that every last ember was dead and cold. It was quite impressive, and the impossible task of conveying thanks to them left me tongue-tied.

While standing numbly next to the spotlight that was trained on the fireman who was poking around the top of the chimney for a last look, I saw a charred lump in the snow. Ringed in soot was a lady holding a parasol — my Grandmother's quilt.

"Sorry about that," said one of the firefighters, whom I finally recognized as the new neighbour who bought a farm two concessions away last summer.

"We had to use it to smother the smoke in the beginning or it would have been a lot worse."

"Never mind," I told him, feeling guilty that sentiment for a blanket could congeal in my mind when he and his mates had risked life and limb to save the roof over my head.

Besides, I have always known that Grandmother's quilt was very special, almost magical in some way. Now it had helped save my house. She would have liked that.

In the aftermath of the fire, that particular Christmas kind of got lost. The insurance adjuster, that faceless name that goes with the premium, turned out to be a very nice man named John. Throughout the festive season, a chaos of cheerful workers — dry-wallers, painters, carpenters and cleaners — streamed into the house. Smoke does an amazing amount of damage, but they managed to clear the air and I no longer felt as though I was living inside a barbecue. Ultimately, the house will be better — and safer — for all of their efforts.

Before I warmed up the wok on that Christmas Eve, I was still putting the final trim on the Christmas tree. A bit late, perhaps, but every ornament and every strand of tinsel seemed vividly alive. When I made my final visit to the barn at midnight, I searched the stars for Santa's sleigh, so that I could send him on his way. My chimney had had quite enough visitors that year. The fact that it was still standing was enough of a gift for me.

The Shepherd in Winter

SOME ANIMALS HANDLE COLD WEATHER BETTER THAN others, and that includes human animals. Given a choice, I find that my horses prefer to spend their days outside, unless the wind is particularly vicious. I can be freezing, but they will be happily rolling in the snow.

By mid-winter, the sheep are wearing five inches of wool. Unless there is a blizzard, the barn door is open and they are free to wander in the fields if they choose. Snow can blanket them and they do not even try to shake it off. If you dig your hand down to their soft pink skin, it is as warm as toast.

My fifteen-year-old barn cat, Webster, spends every winter night snoozing on the back of his favourite old ewe. Neither the cat nor the ewe ever so much as sneeze all winter long. And when there is a touch of a thaw on the pond, the geese are on it like a flash, swimming around like happy polar bears.

In the meantime, if my mitten gets so much as damp, my hand feels as though it is stuck in an ice-cream sandwich.

If I do not wear two or three layers of socks my barn boots are perilously loose.

One blustery day, I was casually tossing flakes of hay into the feeders, when I noticed a ewe standing back from the manger while the rest chewed with a vengeance. Then I saw something small and black near her side, which I assumed to be Webster the Cat just waking up. But when it cried out in a high voice — a sound just like a baby wailing "Ma" — I knew it was a lamb.

Further inspection revealed it to be a female lamb, just hours old. She was dry, fed, warm and bright-eyed. The temperature transition from womb to barn must have been extreme; no one seemed worse for the wear.

I put the pair in a pen and the lamb curled up beside her mother in the straw to have a snooze without so much as a shiver. Transmogrification being what it is, I was tempted to run to the house to make her a hot water bottle to sleep with. But, unlike me, the lamb was thriving with just a simple layer of natural wool to keep out the cold; adding heat would just upset the balance of what nature had her prepared for.

The first time I had lambs born in the winter, I felt so sorry for them that I dashed off to the local thrift store and bought a stockpile of infant undershirts. I had outfitted about a dozen lambs in striped pullovers and pyjama tops imprinted with teddy bears when a local farmer stopped by and put an end to my foolishness.

"If they were meant to come with a suitcase full of clothes, they'd come that way," he announced. "What do you think they have wool for, anyway?"

Although the new ewe lamb adapted with ease, I

considered her to be an accident. A good shepherd should have a management plan, and mine was to avoid subzero lambing — for the good of my own health. I went back to my warm kitchen to blow my nose and check my diary. Sure enough, on or about August the 20th for one brief but seminal moment, the ram had managed to escape from isolation. Obviously, his mission was romance.

I spent that afternoon on my hands and knees checking udders. In the event that the ram had managed to commit bigamy or polygamy, I wanted to be ready. Sheep cannot kick sideways the way a steer can and they do not pack nearly the wallop of a horse's hoof, but they will not line up quietly like dairy cows to have their udders fondled. Instead, they must be coerced into a narrow alleyway where they can be isolated briefly for purposes of medication or, in my case, palpitation.

Every once in a while, one would give a little jump and I would apologize while warming my frosty hands in my mitts for the next one. The only time I came in contact with anything unusual was when the ram slipped through. Oops. He did not like that much.

From the feel of things, it was apparent that only one accident had occurred.

Every time I see the ewe lamb running circles around her mother, I should be reminded of my failure to conduct myself as a proper shepherd and stick to my management plan to have lambs born in April.

Instead, I find myself spending a bit more time in the barn every day — watching her play, and checking to make sure she is settled and comfy when the wind howls at night. Webster sometimes curls up with her or sleeps on top of her mother. No duvets, no fossil fuels, no chicken soup required.

Even in the dead of winter, nature knows best how to take care of its own.

An Inventory
of Mixed Blessings

ON A FARM, NEW YEAR'S DAY IS TRADITIONALLY Inventory Day, and if you do not start the day with a headache, you are headed for one by the end of it. I have resolved to getting the thing over with, and that is my only New Year's resolution. I like to think that my Uncle Ed, who was a real farmer all his life, would be proud to see me out there taking stock of the stock, counting bales of hay and straw and trying to assess grain tonnage.

The sheep have no idea why I spend a whole day in the barn with them, counting their heads. They do not understand about inventory. They are inventory. And sheep don't make New Year's resolutions. Why would they? They don't even know what year it is.

Ah, but if they could, I can think of a few things I would like them to work on as we coast toward the end of the millennium. For instance, maybe, just maybe, they could develop something approximating table manners instead of behaving like convicts at a prison riot when they see me coming with the grain bucket. And maybe they could pause to chew all of their hay and lick their lips clean before they put their muzzles in the water trough and muddle it with dried grasses that I have to scoop out by hand.

There are so many simple things that I wish they would consider changing. After all these years, you would think that they know that only three sheep at a time fit through the gate that leads to the barnyard, but every time the gate is opened five sheep try to jam through. It is not as though I am opening the door to paradise. Once they get to the other side, they generally all want to go back where they came from.

I know that sheep grow up with the notion that the whole world is their lavatory, but I do wish that they could consider controlling themselves when their wool is being sheared. And I do not understand why they think that they should all feel the call of nature whenever I get out the camera.

At least, sheep are never vicious. Even rams do not mean to flatten you when they decide to butt for no apparent reason. To them it is play, and let the shepherd beware.

But my wild tom turkey, Bourbon, has no excuse for attacking me. I wish he would resolve to stop treating me as a target.

I have known this bird since he was an egg. Bourbon was only a week old when he first pecked me, and he has not stopped trying for all of his four years. I have built him a split-level cage with perches high and low and a view of the fields that is as good as my own. I gave him a hen named Blanche to be his mate and friend. But if I so much as stroll by his pen...

When I replenish his feeder, I enter the pen with a garbage can lid to use as a shield. True to his breeding he goes wild — lashing out with wings so strong they can bruise. The pen door may be wide open, but Bourbon will not even try to fly to freedom as long as there is any possibility of putting a dent in me. When I clean his pen, I hustle him outside and he gobbles at the door, waiting to jump back in and attack me. He is too tough an old bird for me to resolve in the roast pan. So I will have to hope that Bourbon's millennial resolution involves turkey-shepherd detente.

You might expect some peace and quiet on a farm, but it does not work that way. I know a certain plumber who would probably like all of my guinea fowl to take a deep, permanent vow of silence.

Anything new or different — from a plumber to a gust of wind — sends guinea fowl into a cacophony of sound. They do not cluck softly like chickens or get it all over with in one great bellowing crow like roosters. Instead guineas have a shrill squawk, dominated by the females cackling, which sounds like a non-stop repetition of the word "buckwheat." Although I begged them to be quiet, those birds "buckwheated" for two solid hours while poor Tom the Plumber wrestled my water pipes into submission. A good plumber is harder to replace than a few guinea fowl.

In my perfectly resolved farm world, geese would not hiss or chase small children. Horses would never swat their tails near burdock bushes. Cats would play with dogs. Cows would resist the temptation of green apples and squirrels would eat the nuts they should have stored for winter instead of raiding the bird feeders.

Imperfection is nothing more than the nature of the beasts. The new year will see a whole new crop of everything on the farm — fresh starts at life and four whole seasons to make this year better than the last. Maybe I will widen the darn barnyard gate so that five sheep can fit through it, since it means so much to them. And maybe while I am taking inventory, I will take some time to count my blessings instead of sheep. That may be the best coping mechanism for a New Year's Day headache.

There's No Loon in My Soup

IN THE CITY, EVERY KIND OF FOOD SEEMS TO BE AVAILABLE all year long. If there is a stalk of asparagus growing somewhere in the world in the middle of darkest January, some clever restaurateur will have it plucked, flown in and served on a big plate with a slice of lemon and a sprig of chervil. Roads can be closed, snow can be piled almost to the tops of telephone poles, but when you wander through an urban supermarket you can find a plump fennel bulb, an eggplant and cobs of sweet corn. But baby beets, bright red peppers, smooth white endive, even radishes that *schmeck* are items that do not turn up at my local produce counter in the middle of winter.

Sometimes it is a challenge trying to find lettuce in flavours other than iceberg.

Sure it is great in the summertime to announce to the world that you are "living out of the garden," but in the winter it is no fun to admit to a steady diet of root vegetables. Forget about chocolate eclairs — in the dark days of February my idea of a treat is pasta dressed with the tomato and basil sauce that I froze in the summer when the tomatoes were red and juicy instead of pink and rock hard.

On mornings when I find that ice rain has coated the tree branches like liquid crystal, I run to the freezer to cherish that last baggie of strawberries picked in July.

If I close my eyes, I can recall a sea of tight-curled fiddleheads growing at the edge of the forest, waving in a spring breeze. And wild leeks. Only in the gloom of winter can one possibly have positive thoughts about those pungent, lingering stink rods.

Call me a masochist, but during the winter-food doldrums my favourite nighttime reading is cookbooks. Oh please, tell me that someday I will make an arugula soufflé. Salsa, I can do that. I waft off to sleep savouring Julia Child's instructions on how to eat an artichoke. In my dreams, Mark Twain holds my hand and reminds me, "When one has tasted watermelon, he knows what the angels eat."

It is an event when something new appears at the produce counter. One week a pile of rock hard avocados arrived. I could ripen them, I knew I could. *The Joy of Cooking* suggested putting them in a paper bag. Julia said room temperature. Someone else suggested burying them in flour overnight. I had frozen raspberries. I could make avocado with raspberry vinaigrette and crème fraîche! I tried all three ripening techniques and turned up mush.

Then one week came the ultimate food distraction. Neat little packages of bright green zucchinis perched beside cabbages. It is common knowledge that zucchini has virtually no taste. Julia simmers it in vermouth to jump start some semblance of flavour. Still, if it was sauteed with garlic and onions and sprinkled with Parmesan cheese, it would make a feast.

But not at $3.99 a pound. I checked the label again. I checked the signage. It *was* $3.99 a pound. Zucchini is mostly water, for goodness' sake. I stood in awe, holding two zucchini with a price tag of $4.56.

It was Seniors' Day at the supermarket. The bus was parked outside, and the free coffee was brewing across from the deli counter. An elderly lady next to me was busily squeezing the wax off a turnip.

"The zucchini is $3.99 a pound," I said, still stunned. I showed her the package.

Another couple of oldsters came along and we all joined carts in the worship and wonder of the $3.99 per pound zucchini.

"You can't give them away in the summer," tsskd the lady in a blue coat with a Persian lamb collar.

"Don't even know how to cook 'em," said a sprightly geezer in a lumberjack jacket.

The young fellow who rotates the cucumbers in the produce section came along and we asked him if there had been an error.

"I always spell zucchini wrong," he said and he took away the sign for correction.

By this time, a thousand years' worth of citizens had congregated at the produce counter.

"If we plant the seeds, maybe we could all afford to retire," said one gnomish woman with a perm so tight that it looked like a Chia pet.

We started giggling. Then we were laughing. Someone

tried to steady themselves on the grapefruits and the whole lot came tumbling down. By the time the produce manager came back with his revised spelling, the guy in the lumberjack jacket was trying to auction off brussels sprouts to the highest bidder and the turnip squeezer was juggling woody parsnips and humming "Yes, We Have No Bananas."

Finally, we all went back to shopping. Nobody bought zucchini.

On the way home, I remembered an odd recipe I found in *The Eskimo Cookbook*. Under the heading "Loon Soup" it said simply, "Do not make loon soup."

Sometimes, even when food is fresh and available, it is just not worth it.

Here Comes the Judge

I DO NOT KNOW WHO SUGGESTED THAT I JUDGE THE snowmobilers' chili contest, but if I ever find out my revenge will be the reverse of the ancient Sicilian adage "revenge is a dish best served cold." Balderdash. My revenge will be swift, and served hot, very hot, at least as hot as chili pot Number 17.

There were twenty-eight Crock-Pots laden with chili when I arrived at the tasting — nary a snowmobiler's helmet in sight. The jolly trailblazers were all out zooming over their carefully groomed trails in packs that sounded like a jet airplane accelerating down a twisted runway.

I was watching the chili co-ordinators connect a dazzling array of extension cords and multi-plugs to the Crock-Pots when my co-adjudicator arrived.

"Call me Ted," said the politician, who is the local sitting Member of Provincial Parliament. Then he promptly sat down.

I could understand why Ted had been anointed as a chili judge. Community service is part of political life and most of what politicians do involves bilious bursts of hot air and laying the blame on others.

I guess I was selected because everyone knows sheep hibernate for the winter and writers are always game for a free lunch. My only experience with snowmobiles ended decades earlier when the one I was a passenger on, an ancient Bombardier infernality, stopped dead in the middle of a frozen corn field — far, far away. Then and there, I took an oath that I would rather be stuck on a horse in a snowdrift any time. Unrelated, unprejudiced and able to swallow seemed to be the criteria for selecting me as a judge.

Fortunately, politicians are masters at these things. "Call-me-Ted" had obviously been to a few goat ropings. On top of first, second and third categories, he added three more potential vote getters — hottest, best looking, and most politically correct. We had two hours, four jugs of water and a box of unsalted crackers to get us through the job.

Each pot was numbered and the ingredients were carefully listed on the back. The organizers had specifically checked each entry to make sure that none of the ingredient lists contained subliminal messages, threats or specific pleas for consideration.

I did note that phrases such as "liberal sprinkling of" managed to compromise some of their best efforts. Ted agreed to ignore such self-defeating chicanery.

We started off on a lovely pot of chili — an ambrosia of beans and meat chunks in a sauce that clung to the wooden spoon with an easy grace. We swallowed. The finish of the chili had an appropriate rise in temperature that burst on the taste buds without damaging the will to continue. Ted gave me one of those "need we go on" looks. Nevertheless, we marked our scorecards rating the chili on a scale of one to five in categories ranging from texture to heat units.

And so it proceeded down the line. There were thick chilies and runny chilies. Chilies with chunks of tomatoes and chilies with catsup-flavoured sauce. Some had lots of meat, some had very little and a couple had no carne at all.

There were kidney beans, lima beans, pinto beans, chickpeas and baked beans from a tin.

One chili even had noodles.

The spicing ranged from brown-sugar sweet to scorching. Ted and I learned to identify deadly hot jalapeno pepper pods. We wrapped them in our napkins when no one was looking, but there was no avoiding the soft-tissue damage inflicted by combinations of cayenne, Tabasco and some concoction called Dan T's Inferno. One chili had sweet pickle in it, another was adrift with baby corn cobs. Some had nuts. But the strangest chili of all was one that had sauerkraut as its secret ingredient. Cruel lot those snowmobiling enthusiasts.

We ended up awarding the grand prize to a chili that smelled darkly of beer. In fact, I think we only settled on it in the end because we were tired of swilling down chili with water.

Coincidentally — or not, perhaps — the winning chili was the masterwork of the town newspaper photographer, so Ted and I were guaranteed front page coverage.

The hottest chili was the two-alarm, arsonist's delight in Crock-Pot 17. It had a unique ability to cause the eyes to water and the toes to curl. The most beautiful was the first pot we gazed upon in all naiveté, and the most politically correct was vegetarian.

The snowmobilers arrived in time for the ceremony. I was slumped over a table covered with cracker crumbs, but Ted was still perky enough to pass comment on the great Canadian tradition of chili-making which unites our nation in both and several languages.

The aftermath of the judging was predictable enough. I am sure the house needed a new roof anyway. I will not be judging such contests in the near future, but I do have a better understanding of what fuels politicians to filibuster. And I will never again describe a cold day as — that word.

Solving a Clear and Present Danger

BIRDS AND GLASS ARE AN UNNATURAL COMBINATION, but every winter they are bound to meet with disastrous results, usually for the birds. The resident chickadees, blue jays, nuthatches and cardinals consider the bird feeders their personal fast food drive-thru. They know where the outdoors ends and the glass begins on the windows that overlook their feeders. It is the newcomers and migrating flocks touching down for a quick feed who tend to confront glass head-on.

The sound of a bird hitting glass is distinctive — a dull thump rather than a crash. Sometimes the crasher flies off before it can even be located. Other times there is a period of head shaking and a general shutdown of bird-like activity, as though the creature is checking to see if all systems are still a "go."

A barn owl once shot clear through a friend's garage window and it spent the whole day regrouping in an old laundry basket. His Wiseness's only movement was the rotation of his head to observe his host's every movement.

After a day at the recuperation station, he flew away.

Victims of head-on-window-collisions are not always so fortunate. With the exception of installing STOP signs over the exterior of the house, it seemed impossible to warn the birds without cluttering up the view of them. I knew that they were not banging into the window because they wanted to watch television. It was just a matter of finding some way to warn them that they could understand at a distance.

Oddly, the solution was an owl — a huge, stuffed horned owl posed in mid-air with its talons in attack mode and its wings spread. Even birds who pal with owls would have to find this thing as scary as Jabba the Hut.

A taxidermist who lives in the North had stuffed the road-killed beauty for practice. Transferring the bird to me involved letters of permit and all sorts of administrative jumble. In this country, it may be easier to keep grandfather stuffed on the couch collecting pension cheques than it is to put an accidentally deceased bird of prey in a window to ward off headaches in juncos.

The owl is perched at the side of one window on top of a stereo speaker, a stance it would hardly take in real life. Still, even the sunflower-seed-crazed blue jays kept their distance until finally it filtered through their bird brains that the owl was not moving, not going anyone's way, neither a fellow traveller nor a threat to the niger seed.

The owl certainly gives newcomers pause. When migrating flocks come through, the leader is generally wary enough to scout the zone and spot the owl. Instead of grazing within its "sight," they choose the feeders at the side of the house, where the windows are smaller and much easier to identify. It is a win-win situation.

The natural habitat of birds does not include plastic gazebos filled with food and rendered lard does not sprout seeds of its own accord. However, in the popular culture of birds, anything containing seeds or suet is as obvious in the landscape as an Inuit *inukshuk* marking a route once travelled. Survival accommodates unnatural combinations.

Come to think of it, I never in my wildest dreams ever imagined that I would be dusting a dead owl in my living room to ward off thumps on the windows.

Spring Will Be Sprung

*W*HEN IT IS TIME FOR WINTER TO BE OVER, I DO NOT need a groundhog to give me a date. Every living thing seems to have an opinion.

I was at the Holstein Feed Mill the other day. It is as much a place about "what's going on" as "what are you going to feed the pigs?" One of the senior farmers was holding court next to a pile of blue salt licks that lined the wall and made a perfect jumping ground for half a dozen calico kittens.

"March is going to be a cold one," he announced.

I shivered in my toque.

"But in April we'll all be wearing shorts," he said, confidently, digging his hands deep in his pockets and lowering his chin to his collar.

Good news at last. I had visions of greening fields and planting early radishes, peas, onions and carrots. I rushed home and started the tomatoes in a flat beside the sunniest window in the house.

Animals tell you when the season is going to turn. My

gaggle of geese is never about to keep quiet when they feel a change coming on. They are out there falling in love left, right and centre. It is a hissing and honking ritual that hardly smacks of the poetry of love, but the ganders are gradually staking their claim to the females. One old layer is already gathering materials for her nest.

As the days get longer, the chickens start laying eggs. Nothing organized mind you. Every once in a while I will pull a bale of hay from the top of the pile and an egg will drop. Sometimes it's a freshly laid egg, so I scramble to catch whatever I can before it scrambles itself.

I might get a touch of cabin fever waiting for the weather to break, but so does the livestock.

I once had a Hereford cow named Hazel who gave birth to her calf in a snowbank in the middle of winter. A month later, she took off over the fields with the little guy at her heels and ended up camping out beside a dairy barn.

"I think she needs the bull," said the Mennonite man who found her.

That is a sure sign of spring.

When old Lady the horse gets bored, I take her out for a walk to the end of the lane. Then her daughter Karma wants the same change of scenery. Both of them greet me each day like anxious puppies waiting to see what new "activity" I have planned for them. If they are lucky enough to be at the bottom of the lane when the snowplough goes by, it makes their day.

Once the ice melts, I can take them on trail rides. It will not be long, because when I groom them, handfuls of their shaggy winter coats come out in the brushing, but I am still wearing long johns.

In the meantime, I can get a head start on renovating a little pasture where a few ancient apple trees still provide a bounty of fruit. It is a hilly and bumpy plot of ground, too rough for regular ploughing. So, I go out and toss clover seed on the snow, in the hopes that a spring thaw will take the seed down into the earth and add a touch of goodness for the sheep to chew on in the fall.

"Frost seeding," they call it at the feed mill. It is hard to believe that such tiny seeds can survive in such miserably cold weather, but doing it makes me feel better. And "I'm Looking Over a Four-Leaf Clover" sounds great on the old kazoo.

When March comes in like a lion and goes out like a lamb, it means I am headed straight into an April that is filled with lambs. The sheep grow round and full with a bounty of babies. Through it all, there is a delightful calming that comes over them, balancing the constant honking antics of the hormone-crazed geese and the anxious prancing of the horses.

I can accept that to every season there is a time and a purpose. But just in case the farmer at the feed mill is right, I have been nosing through the summer clothes. When the warm day dawns that I can wear shorts again, I will be ready.